NUGGETS YOU ARE A PRECIOUS JEWEL

BY SHERELYN DUHART

Copyright 2012 all rights reserved

Library of Congress

Author, Sherelyn Duhart

ISBN: 978-0-9822468-4-9

www.duhartpress.com

Duhart Press, LLC

Edited by Editor World

Artwork by Gary Tenant

In memory of my mother,

Maurice Duhart, a precious jewel. Thanks for your support and just being an angel to me.

YOU ARE BEAUTIFUL

Psalms 139:13-14—For thou hast covered me in my mother's womb. I will praise thee; for I am fearfully and wonderfully made: marvelous are thy works; and that my soul knoweth right well.

You are an original masterpiece designed by God. He wants you to have high thoughts of yourself. You are a precious jewel, just like the diamonds, sapphires, and rubies.

NOTES FOR
YOU ARE BEAUTIFUL

DO YOU HAVE VIRTUE?

Proverbs 31:10   Who can find a virtuous woman? For her price is far above rubies.

The virtuous woman sounds like a super hero. God will show you how your virtue will shine. What must you do to become a virtuous woman? Virtue means strength, efficiency, and ability. It is strength of character, which is moral strength and firmness. Ruth in the Bible is considered a virtuous woman. She feared God, loved the truth, and hated sin. In today's world, people are morally weak and so anemic in character, when a woman or man of strength shows up it is obvious to all.

NOTES FOR

DO YOU HAVE VIRTUE?

DO YOU KNOW WHY YOU WERE CREATED?

Proverbs 19:21—Many are the plans in a person's heart, but it is the Lord's purpose that prevails. (NIV)

You might be called to be a housewife, a school teacher, a doctor, or an encourager. Whatever it is God wants you to do, do it wholeheartedly with passion. When you know why you were created, you are focused. God will show you what you are supposed to do in life. You must delight yourself in him. In the Bible, Esther, Ruth, Naomi, Deborah, Sarah, and Mary walked in the purposes of God. Esther saved the Jews. Ruth served Naomi. Deborah won a war. Mary gave birth to Jesus. What is your purpose?

NOTES FOR
DO YOU KNOW
WHY YOU WERE CREATED?

ARE YOU ALWAYS COMPARING?

James 3:16–For where envying and strife is, there is confusion and every evil work.

Proverbs 14:30– A heart at peace gives life to the body, but envy rots the bones. (NIV)

Do you say my house is bigger than hers? I drive a newer car. You need to lose weight or I look better than you. I am finer than you. My hair is prettier than yours.

All comparing is a waste of time and shallow. No one has the same bills or the exact situation. The look thing is ludicrous. God is creative, so to compare hair, size, and looks, is so ridiculous. We have to take a look at ourselves and ask what makes me compare myself with others. Are you happy with yourself?

NOTES FOR ARE

YOU ALWAYS COMPARING?

DO YOU TRUST GOD?

Proverbs 3:5–Trust in the Lord with all thine heart; and lean not unto thine own understanding.

God is faithful. He answers prayers. Sometimes we have to wait. Waiting on God takes faith. Faith is nothing that you see. Can you trust him? Will you trust him? He gives good and perfect gifts. A perfect gift can be peace, healthy relationships, good health–not just things.

NOTES FOR

DO YOU TRUST GOD?

WILL YOU BE THE OTHER WOMAN?

Exodus 20:14—Thou shalt not commit adultery.

Being the other woman is nothing new. Some people do not mind being the other woman as long as they are the only other woman. Do you really want to be second best? How many men do you know have actually divorced their wives for their mistress? This triangle ends up having a lot of confusion. Some people end up being stalkers and sometimes dead. If you are legally married but separated you are still committing adultery. We have to obey the laws of the land, and God's law.

NOTES FOR WILL YOU BE THE OTHER WOMAN ?

ARE YOU CREATING EMOTIONAL TIES?

1 Corinthians 6:18-20–Flee fornication. Every sin that a man doeth is without the body; but he that committeth fornication sinneth against his own body. What? Know ye not that your body is the temple of the Holy Ghost which is in you, which ye have of God, and ye are not your own? For ye are bought with a price: therefore glorify God in your body, and in your spirit, which are God's.

ARE YOU CREATING EMOTIONAL TIES? (CONTINUED)

Sex is rampant in the world today. You do not have to be married. Forget about marriage. You can get it whenever, however, and whatever way you want. What does God have to say about it all? His word is still alive and true. Sex is designed for you to become one with your spouse. That is why the word says the two shall become one. There have been incidents in which people have become violent stalkers because someone did not want to be bothered with them after they had conquered them. What emotional ties are you creating?

NOTES FOR

ARE YOU CREATING EMOTIONAL TIES?

IS HE TOUCHING YOU?

1 Corinthians 7:1-2, 9–Now concerning the things whereof ye wrote unto me: It is good for a man not to touch a woman. Nevertheless, to avoid fornication, let every man have his own wife, and let every woman have her own husband. But if they cannot contain, let them marry, for it is better to marry than to burn.

Sex is so common. If you are a child of God, you are called to wait. In society today, it is hard, but you can wait on the Lord. You have so much peace when you wait on the Lord. You have less drama when you wait on the Lord.

NOTES FOR

IS HE TOUCHING YOU?

ARE YOU A GOSSIP?

Proverbs 11:13– A talebearer revealeth secrets: but he that is of a faithful spirit concealeth the matter.

Proverbs 18:8–The words of a talebearer are as wounds, and they go down into the innermost parts of the belly.

Proverbs 16:28– A perverse person stirs up conflict, and a gossip separates close friends. (NIV)

ARE YOU A GOSSIP? (CONTINUED)

Proverbs 26:20–Without wood a fire goes out; without a gossip a quarrel dies down. (NIV)

Do you know everyone's business? Do you share your friends', coworkers', and relatives' business? Gossiping creates confusion. Why do you gossip? If you gossip, are you happy with yourself?

NOTES FOR

ARE YOU A GOSSIP?

WHO ARE YOU LOYAL TO?

Ruth 1:16–And Ruth said, Intreat me not to leave thee, or to return from following after thee: for whither thou goest, I will go; and where thou lodgest, I will lodge: thy people shall be my people, and thy God my God.

Proverbs 27:9–Just as lotions and fragrance give sensual delight, a sweet friendship refreshes the soul. (MSG)

WHO ARE YOU LOYAL TO? (CONTINUED)

Ruth was very loyal to her mother-in-law, even after her husband died. She told Naomi she would follow her and her Lord would be her Lord. Her desire was to be loyal to Naomi.

When was the last time you were loyal? Who do you respect? Do you consider others? Do you talk about your friends behind their back?

NOTES FOR
WHO ARE YOU
LOYAL TO?

ARE YOU WEARY?

Galatians 6:9–And let us not be weary in well doing: for in due season we shall reap, if we faint not.

Are you looking for a job? Have you been unemployed for more than a year? Did you lose a loved one?

Sometimes you have to wait for that job to come. Do not stop looking. God will bless you. You will find that God takes care of your daily needs, no matter what economic state you are in. God is faithful. As the days go by, crying will slow down over the loss of a loved one. There will always be great memories.

NOTES FOR
ARE YOU WEARY?

ARE YOU HAPPY FOR YOUR FRIEND?

Deuteronomy 5:21—Neither shalt thou desire thy neighbour's wife; neither shalt thou covet thy neighbor's house, his field, or his manservant, or his maidservant, his ox, or his ass, or anything that is thy neighbour's.

Your time will come to get the house, the car, the spouse, the business, or whatever. God wants to bless you. The steps of a good man are ordered by the Lord. Everyone's steps are not the same. Just be happy for others. Do not hate or envy.

NOTES FOR

ARE YOU HAPPY FOR YOUR FRIEND?

ARE YOU IN DENIAL?

1 Thessalonians 4:11—And that ye study to be quiet, and to do your own business, and to work with your own hands.

Are you a mess-starter? Do you start confusion and then act like you are innocent? Would you be offended if someone started trouble with you? For example, do you talk about Sally to Jane, and then go to Sally and talk about Jane? You are starting a fire, especially if these girls do not like each other. Why do you do what you do? Most people have enough business of their own to take care of. Women, we should consider our ways. Why would you instigate? Are you happy with yourself?

NOTES FOR
ARE YOU IN DENIAL?

MONEY

1 Timothy 6:10–For the love of money is a root of all kinds of evil. Some people, eager for money, have wondered from the faith and pierced themselves with grief. (NIV)

Money has caused many problems for people. Disagreements occur. It is a process in learning to be a wise steward of your money. God can help you with that. Keeping up with the Joneses or the Smiths can be expensive. Living above your means can be painful. Worrying about money can cause you to lose sleep and have no peace.

NOTES FOR

MONEY

ARE YOU THE ANGRY SISTER?

Ephesians 4:26–Be ye angry, and sin not: let not the sun go down upon your wrath.

Proverbs 16:32–Better a patient person than a warrior, one with self-control than one who takes a city. (NIV)

Ecclesiastes 7:9–Be not hasty in thy spirit to be angry: for anger resteth in the bosom of fools.

ARE YOU THE ANGRY SISTER (CONTINUED)

Are you the sister who cannot communicate when there is a conflict? Are you your own worst enemy? Do you have uncontrolled anger? Do you harm yourself when you are angry? Sometimes we just have to calm down. It is not that serious. Do you act crazy because someone accidentally harmed your computer, your iPod, your cell phone, your car, or wasted something on you?

NOTES FOR

ARE YOU THE ANGRY SISTER?

ARE YOU THE SCARY SISTER?

2 Timothy 1:7—For God hath not given us the spirit of fear; but of power, and of love, and of a sound mind.

Hebrews 13:6—So that we may boldly say, The Lord is my helper, and I will not fear what man shall do unto me.

John 14:27—Peace I leave with you, my peace I give unto you: not as the world giveth, give I unto you. Let not your heart be troubled, neither let it be afraid.

ARE YOU THE SCARY SISTER (CONTINUED)

Don't be afraid to speak up, God is with you. Take him with you wherever you go. Trust God. He will never leave you or forsake you. He will give you peace in the midst of the storm. Are you scared to make a stand in the presence of your enemies? Once you try it, you will see that you can trust God and relax more.

NOTES FOR

ARE YOU THE SCARY SISTER?

LOOKING FOR LOVE IN ALL THE WRONG PLACES

John 15:13-14— Greater love hath no man than this, that a man lay down his life for his friends. Ye are my friends, if ye do whatsoever I command you.

Are you looking for love in people that are not even thinking about you? Are you always looking for validation? Are you secure in yourself?

Rest in the Lord. He will validate you. There is love and acceptance in Jesus.

NOTES FOR

LOOKING FOR LOVE IN ALL THE WRONG PLACES?

SHUN THE APPEARANCE!

1 Thessalonians 5:22—Abstain from all appearance of evil.

Do not be a partaker. We are living in a crazy world. Use God's wisdom when you are flirting with something or someone that does not lawfully belong to you. The consequences can be severe: you might get jail time, or maybe death. Unhealthy relationships are not good. Christians watch what you do. People are watching. It might be innocent, but remember the word of God says abstain from the appearance of evil.

NOTES FOR

SHUN THE APPEARANCE

DO YOU BUILD UP OR TEAR DOWN?

Proverbs 18:24—A man that hath friends must shew himself friendly: and there is a friend that sticketh closer than a brother.

Do you treat your friends with respect by building them up? Do you throw in slick remarks, attempting to tear people down? Do you say negative things? Do you think about what you say or how you say something? We should encourage and build people up. There are times we should tell them the truth. Most people know when they are not being nice. Treat people how you want to be treated.

NOTES FOR

DO YOU BUILD UP OR TEAR DOWN?

GOING IN CIRCLES?

Mark 9:2—And after six days, Jesus taketh with him Peter, James, and John, and leadeth them up into an high mountain apart by themselves: and he was transfigured before them.

Jesus loved all of his disciples. He knew each and every one of them. He even knew Judas would betray him. Jesus shows you how to walk in love. He even shows us that some people will be closer than others. You will know who should be the hello, the casual, the associate, or the real friends. God is faithful. Peter, James, and John got special attention from Jesus. Are you going in circles with friendships or relationships?

NOTES FOR
GOING IN CIRCLES

CHECK IT OUT!

Luke 14:28–For which of you, intending to build a tower, does not sit down first and count the cost, whether he has enough to finish it– (NKJV)

The word of God says count the cost.

Before you purchase, invest, or get yoked up.

Check out how much it cost in the short run and the long run. Pray about it. God sends confirmation to what he has shown you. He gives you peace when it is the right decision.

NOTES FOR
CHECK IT OUT

YOU WILL KNOW!!!

1 Peter 5:7–Cast your cares upon him, for he cares for you.

Proverbs 3:6–In all thy ways acknowledge him, and he shall direct thy paths.

When it comes to relationships, he will show you something is wrong. God will let you know. All you have to do is listen.

Something is wrong when a person you want to be with has horrible relationships with everyone. This person is never wrong or never admits to being wrong. They can never say I am sorry or forgive me. You will know, just pay attention.

NOTES FOR
YOU WILL KNOW

YOUR NEEDS?

Proverbs 3:5-6–Trust in the Lord with all your heart, and lean not on your own understanding; in all your ways acknowledge Him, and He shall direct your paths. (NKJV)

The word of God says I will supply your needs according to his riches in glory.

God will provide your needs when you are hungry, in need of money, a job, or whatever else you need. When you serve God he gives you favor. Favor is something God gives you. It can be a job or a promotion, and everyone will wonder how you got it. Some people may not like it. Walk in your favor.

NOTES FOR YOUR NEEDS

YOUR WANTS

Matthew 6:33–But seek ye first the kingdom of God and His righteousness, and all these things shall be added to you. (NKJV)

Psalms 37:4–Delight thyself also in the Lord: and he shall give thee the desires of thine heart.

God is so good. He gives you your daily bread, which are your needs. God can give you your wants. You will know it, because you might say, wow, Lord, I was not even looking for that and you gave that to me. It is exciting. God is faithful.

NOTES FOR YOUR WANTS

IF IT DOES NOT FIT DO NOT FORCE IT!

Matthew 5:16–Let your light so shine before men, that they may see your good works, and glorify your Father which is in heaven.

Dear servant of God, you might feel like an apple around a lot of oranges, bananas or pears. You are called not to fit in. You are a servant of the highest God. You cannot force yourself to fit in. Walk in who you are. You are a child of God showing your light.

NOTES FOR

IF IT DOES NOT FIT

DO NOT FORCE IT

WHAT ARE YOU CONSUMED WITH?

Exodus 20:3—Thou shalt have no other gods before me.

God wants to be first. Have you accepted his son Jesus as your personal Savior? Do you keep your mind on God? What do you focus on? What do you eat, sleep, or drink? What consumes your thoughts twenty-four hours a day?

NOTES FOR

WHAT ARE YOU CONSUMED WITH?

Women in the Bible

THE SAMARITAN WOMAN

John 4:9—Then saith the woman of Samaria unto him, How is that thou, being a Jew, askest drink of me, which am a woman of Samaria? For the Jews have no dealings with the Samaritans.

The woman of Samaria was looked down upon by the Jews because of her nationality. Jesus was not concerned about her race or culture. He talked to the woman regardless of all the prejudices. This woman went to draw water in the heat of the day instead of the evening.

THE SAMARITAN WOMAN (continued)

She did this to avoid the sharp tongues of the women at the well. The custom was to go to the well in the evening. Jesus did the opposite of what everyone else did. He showed love.

Sister, God loves you if you are from North America, South America, Europe, Asia, Africa, Australia, or Antarctica. God is no respecter of persons. Who are we showing love to? Treat people the way you want to be treated.

NOTES FOR THE SAMARITAN WOMAN

LEAH, THE ONE JACOB LOVED LESS

Genesis 29:17-18—Leah was tender eyed; but Rachel was beautiful and well favoured. And Jacob loved Rachel; and said, I will serve thee seven years for Rachel thy younger daughter.

Jacob worked seven years for Rachel. But Laban gave him Leah instead of Rachel. Jacob consummated the marriage but did not realize it was Leah. Jacob was disappointed but willing to work another seven years for Rachel. God saw that Leah was hated, so he blessed her with children.

LEAH, THE ONE JACOB LOVED LESS (CONTINUED)

In those days, it was very important for women to have babies. Leah's womb was opened and Rachel was barren for a long time. She finally had Joseph and Benjamin. Leah's sons included Judah, the ancestor of David the king of Israel and of Jesus the long-awaited Messiah. God favored Leah.

NOTES FOR

LEAH, THE ONE JACOB LOVED LESS

THE WOMAN WITH THE ISSUE OF BLOOD

Mark 5:25-30—And a certain woman, which had an issue of blood twelve years, And had suffered many things of many physicians, and had spent all that she had, and was nothing bettered, but rather grew worse, When she had heard of Jesus, she came in the press behind, and touched his garment. For she said, If I may touch but his clothes, I shall be whole.

THE WOMAN WITH THE ISSUE OF BLOOD

(CONTINUED)

And straightway the fountain of her blood was dried up; and she felt in her body that she was healed of that plague. And Jesus immediately knowing in himself that virtue had gone out of him, turned him about in the press, and said, Who touched my clothes?

The woman with the issue of blood was healed when she touched the hem of Jesus' garment. She acted in faith. Remember that Jesus has the power to heal you. He took thirty-nine stripes for you.

NOTES FOR

THE WOMAN WITH THE ISSUE OF BLOOD

THE WOMAN WHO HUMBLED HERSELF

Luke 7:36-50—One of the Pharisees asked Jesus to come to his home for lunch and Jesus accepted the invitation. As they sat down to eat, a woman of the streets—a prostitute—heard he was there and brought an exquisite flask filled with expensive perfume. Going in, she knelt behind him at his feet, weeping, with her tears falling down upon his feet; and she wiped them off with her hair and kissed them and poured the perfume on them. (TLB)

THE WOMAN WHO HUMBLED HERSELF

(CONTINUED)

The Pharisees did not like the fact that Jesus allowed this woman to wipe his feet with her hair and the perfume. Jesus honored the woman because she did not mind kissing his feet and greeting him. Jesus said her sins are forgiven, because she loved much. Her faith saved her. Jesus told the Pharisees they were not hospitable and they should be humble like this woman. Jesus received from someone most people would talk about. You never know whom God will use.

NOTES FOR

THE WOMAN WHO HUMBLED HERSELF

TAMAR, WHO WAS VIOLATED

2 Samuel 13:11-14—And when she had brought them unto him to eat, he took hold of her, and said unto her, Come lie with me, my sister. And she answered him, Nay, my brother, do not force me; for no such thing ought to be done in Israel. Now therefore, I pray thee, speak unto the king, for he will not withhold thee from thee. Howbeit he would not hearken unto her voice: but, being stronger than she, forced her, and lay with her.

TAMAR, WHO WAS VIOLATED (CONTINUED)

Of course Tamar was upset. She felt violated–and by her brother. Absalom her brother was upset that Amnon raped his sister and he had him killed. You do reap what you sow. Amnon reaped death. God can help you get over this devastation. Forgiveness and love helps us overcome this kind of hurt. Turn your hurt or your pain over to God.

NOTES FOR

TAMAR-WHO WAS VIOLATED

THE DELILAH DEMISE!

Judges 16:4-6–And it came to pass afterward, that he loved a woman in the valley of Sorek, whose name was Delilah. And the lords of the Philistines came up unto her, and said unto her. Entice him, and see wherein his great strength lieth, and by what means we may prevail against him, that we may bind him to afflict him; and we will give thee every one of us eleven hundred pieces of silver. And Delilah said to Samson, Tell me, I pray thee, wherein thy great strength lieth, and wherewith thou mightest be bound to afflict thee.

THE DELILAH DEMISE! (CONTINUED)

Delilah tried several times to get the information about his strength. She made Samson feel bad for not telling her at first. Samson mocked her several times. He finally told her his strength was in his hair. Delilah ordered a servant to cut Samson's hair while he slept. He lost his strength. Eventually Samson's hair grew back. He destroyed the Philistines but died doing so. Delilah was devious and sneaky. She played with Samson's emotions. Samson was strong at first. It seemed like it was over. But he prayed to God. Samson had victory in his death. There is victory when you trust God. Are you a Delilah?

NOTES FOR
THE DELILAH DEMISE!

WHAT DID REBEKAH DO?

Genesis 27:6-7, 11-13–And Rebekah spake unto Jacob her son, saying, Behold, I heard thy father speak unto Esau thy brother, saying, Bring me venison, and make me savoury meat, that I may eat, and bless thee before the Lord before my death.

And Jacob said to Rebekah his mother, Behold, Esau my brother is a hairy man, and I am a smooth man: My father peradventure will feel me, and I shall seem to him as a deceiver; and I shall bring a curse upon me, and not a blessing.

WHAT DID REBEKAH DO? (CONTINUED)

And his mother said unto him, Upon me be thy curse, my son: only obey my voice, and go fetch me them.

Deceiving people will not get you anywhere. Jacob and his mother were wrong for tricking his father and taking Esau's blessings. God did bless Jacob, but first he had to be broken and humbled. Deceitfulness is not of God.

NOTES FOR

WHAT DID REBEKAH DO?

GOD IS FAITHFUL TO ABIGAIL

1 Samuel 25:2-3— And there was a man in Maon, whose possessions were in Carmel; and the man was very great, and he had three thousand sheep, and a thousand goats: and he was shearing his sheep in Carmel. Now the name of the man was Nabal; and the name of his wife Abigail: and she was a woman of good understanding, and of a beautiful countenance: but the man was churlish and evil in his doings.

GOD IS FAITHFUL TO ABIGAIL

(CONTINUED)

Nabal had 3,000 sheep and 1,000 goats. Abigail was a good woman, but Nabal was churlish. This means he was rude and had a bad disposition. He was cruel to Abigail. Nabal died. David married Abigail. David treated her better.

Abigail deserved to be treated as a queen, after being with such a mean man. She withstood all the meanness her first husband dished out. God blessed her.

NOTES FOR

GOD IS FAITHFUL TO ABIGAIL

BATHSHEBA BATHES OPENLY

2 Samuel 11:2-3—And it came to pass in an eveningtide, that David arose from his bed, and walked upon the roof of the king's house: and from the roof he saw a woman washing herself; and the woman was very beautiful to look upon. And David sent and inquired after the woman. And one said, Is this not this Bathsheba, the daughter of Eliam, the wife of Uriah the Hittite?

BATHSHEBA BATHES OPENLY

(CONTINUED)

David lusted after Bathsheba. They had sex; Bathsheba became pregnant. David had Uriah, Bathsheba's husband, killed. It does take two to commit adultery. God was displeased with David's actions. He should not have pursued Bathsheba. David committed adultery and murder. David asked God to give him a clean heart. God is a forgiving God. Watch what you do, our actions have consequences.

NOTES FOR

BATHSHEBA BATHES OPENLY

DON'T BE POWER STRUCK LIKE ATHALIAH!

2 Kings 11:1-2 And when Athaliah the mother of Ahazaiah saw that her son was dead, she arose and destroyed the seed royal. But Jehosheba, the daughter of king Joram, sister of Ahaziah, took Joash the son of Ahaziah, and stole him from among the king's sons which were slain; and they hid him, even him and his nurse, in the bedchamber from Athaliah, so that he was not slain. And he was with her hid in the house of the Lord six years. And Athaliah did reign over the land.

DON'T BE POWER STRUCK LIKE ATHALIAH!

(CONTINUED)

Athaliah was mad because her son was dead and she decided to kill all the royal seed. Her success did not last. God is the avenger, not us. Eventually, the king's son grew up to be king, and his followers captured and killed Athaliah.

Let God fight your battles. The Lord knows we hurt when we lose our loved ones. God can handle it and heal your hurts. Trust God.

NOTES FOR

DON'T BE POWER STRUCK LIKE ATHALIAH!

ESTHER WAS A WOMAN OF PURPOSE

Esther 5:4–"If it pleases the king," replied Esther, "let the king, together with Haman, come today to a banquet I have prepared for him."

Esther 7:6–Esther said, "An adversary and enemy! This vile Haman!" Then Haman was terrified before the king and queen. The king got up in a rage, left his wine and went out into the palace garden. But Haman, realizing that the king had already decided his fate, stayed behind to beg Queen Esther for his life.

ESTHER WAS A WOMAN OF PURPOSE (CONTINUED)

What an awesome task for Esther, to be responsible for saving the Jews. Esther walked in faith. Haman did not like Jews, but all the wrong he planned backfired in his face when Esther requested a meeting with the king. She had enough faith to request her husband the king's attention. God placed Esther in the right position to save the Jews. Trust God–you never know how He is going to work things out.

NOTES FOR

ESTHER WAS A WOMAN OF PURPOSE

DORCAS WAS LOVED BY HER PEERS

Acts 9:36-38—Now there was at Joppa a certain disciple named Tabitha, which by interpretation is called Dorcas: this woman was full of good works and almsdeeds which she did. And it came to pass in those days, that she was sick, and died: whom when thy had washed, they laid her in an upper chamber. And forasmuch as Lydda was nigh to Joppa, and the disciples had heard that Peter was there, they sent unto him two men, desiring him that he would not delay to come to them.

DORCAS WAS LOVED BY HER PEERS

(CONTINUED)

Acts 9:40—But Peter put them all forth, and kneeled down, and prayed; and turning him to the body said, Tabitha, arise. And she opened her eyes: and when she saw Peter, she sat up.

It is great to have friends that want you to come alive after you have died. They begged Peter to come and raise her from the dead. She was a very hospitable person. She made beautiful garments and gave them away.

NOTES FOR

DORCAS WAS LOVED BY HER PEERS

DEBORAH THE GENERAL

Judges 4:14 And Deborah said unto Barak, Up; for this is the day in which the Lord hath delivered Sisera into thine hand: is not the Lord gone out before thee? So Barak went down from mount Tabor, and ten thousand men after him.

Together, Deborah and Barak beat Sisera. Deborah, a woman in charge of a nation, walked in her purpose. She was bold in God. God gave her an awesome task.

NOTES FOR

DEBORAH THE GENERAL

MARY!

Luke 1:30-32 And the angel said unto her, Fear not, Mary: for thou hast found favour with God. And behold, thou shalt conceive in thy womb, and bring forth a son, and shalt call his name Jesus. He shall be great, and shall be called the Son of the Highest: and the Lord God shall give unto him the throne of his father David.

Luke 1:34-35 Then said Mary unto the angel, How shall this be, seeing I know not a man? And the angel answered and said unto her,

MARY!

(CONTINUED)

The Holy Ghost shall come upon thee, and the power of the Highest shall overshadow thee: therefore also that holy thing which shall be born of thee shall be called the Son of God.

Mary the mother of Jesus was a virgin. She accepted the fact that she carried the Savior. She accepted the call when she said, Be it unto me according to thy word. What awesome thing, to be the mother of Jesus!

NOTES FOR MARY!

QUEEN SHEBA

1 Kings 10:1-2—When the queen of Sheba heard about the fame of Solomon and his relation to the name of the Lord, she came to test him with hard questions. Arriving at Jerusalem with a very great caravan—with camels carrying spices, large quantities of gold, and precious stones—she came to Solomon and talked with him about all that she had on her mind.

1 Kings 10:6-7—She said to the king, "The report I heard in my own country about your achievements and your wisdom is true. 7 But I did not believe these things until I came and saw with my own eyes. Indeed, not even half was told me; in wisdom and

QUEEN SHEBA

(CONTINUED)

wealth you have far exceeded the report I heard.

1 Kings 10:10—And she gave the king 120 talents of gold, large quantities of spices, and precious stones. Never again were so many spices brought in as those the queen of Sheba gave to King Solomon.

Queen Sheba shared her gifts after she realized what Solomon was all about. She did not believe it at first. That was a selfless act to give him the gifts she gave.

NOTES FOR
QUEEN SHEBA

HANNAH KEEPS HER PROMISE

1 Samuel 1:11, 20, 27-28—And she made a vow, saying, "O Lord Almighty, if you will only look upon your servant's misery and remember me, and not forget your servant but give her a son, then I will give him to the Lord for all the days of his life, and no razor will ever be used on his head." So in the course of time Hannah conceived and gave birth to a son. She named him Samuel, saying, because I asked the Lord for him." I prayed for this child, and the Lord has granted me what I asked of him.

HANNAH KEEPS HER PROMISE

(CONTINUED)

So now I give him to the Lord. For his whole life he will be given over to the Lord." And he worshiped the Lord there.

Hannah made a promise to God that she would dedicate her son to the Lord if he gave her one. She kept that vow. God answered her prayer. She was a woman of her word.

NOTES FOR

HANNAH KEEPS HER PROMISE

JEHOSHEBA-A BRAVE WOMAN

2 Chronicles 22:10-12—When Athaliah the mother of Ahaziah saw that her son was dead; she proceeded to destroy the whole royal family of the house of Judah. But Jehosheba, the daughter of King Jehoram, took Joash son Ahaziah and stole him away from among the royal princes who were about to be murdered and put him and his nurse in a bedroom.

JEHOSHEBA-A BRAVE WOMAN

(CONTINUED)

Because Jehosheba, the daughter of King Jehoram and wife of the priest Jehoiada, was Ahaziah's sister, she hid the child from Athaliah so she could not kill him. He remained hidden with them at the temple of God for six years while Athaliah ruled the land. (NIV)

Jehosheba was a bold woman in the midst of all the chaos. She was a woman of faith; it would have been easy to be overtaken with fear.

NOTES FOR

JEHOSHEBA-A BRAVE WOMAN

LYDIA-WHAT A LADY

Acts 16:13-15—On the Sabbath we went outside the city gate to the river, where we expected to find a place of prayer. We sat down and began to speak to the women who had gathered there. One of those listening was a woman named Lydia, a dealer in purple cloth from the city of Thyatira, who was a worshiper of God. The Lord opened her heart to respond to Paul's message.

LYDIA-WHAT A LADY (CONTINUED)

"When she and the members of their household were baptized, she invited us to her home. "If you consider me a believer in the Lord, "she said " come and stay at my house." And she persuaded us. (NIV)

Lydia had the gift of hospitality and was a successful businesswoman who sold cloth. She showed hospitality to Paul and Silas before they were imprisoned. Paul was her guest after he was imprisoned. Lydia was Paul's first convert and the first member of the church at Phillipi. Lydia was all about God's business.

NOTES FOR

LYDIA-WHAT A LADY

MIRIAM PRAISED THE LORD

Exodus 15:20-22—And Miriam the prophetess, the sister of Aaron, took a timbrel in her hand; and all the women went out after her with timbrels and with dances. And Miriam answered them, Sing ye to the Lord, for he hath triumphed gloriously, the horse and his rider hath he thrown into the sea. So Moses brought Israel from the Red Sea, and they went out into the wilderness of Shur; and they went three days in the wilderness, and found no water.

Miriam led the celebration after crossing the Red Sea. She was a worshipper. She delivered God's message to the people.

NOTES FOR

MIRIAM PRAISED THE LORD

HULDAH-A PROPHETESS

2 Kings 22:14-16—Hilkiah the priest, and Ahikam, Acbor, Shaphan and Asaiah went to speak to the prophetess Huldah, who was the wife of Shallum son of Tikvah, the son of Harhas, keeper of the wardrobe. She lived in Jerusalem, in the Second District. She said to them, This is what the Lord, the God of Israel, says: Tell the man who sent you to me, "This is what the Lord says: I am going to bring disaster on this place and its people, according to everything written in the book the king of Judah has read.

HULDAH-A PROPHETESS
(CONTINUED)

She obeyed God by prophesying to the people and warning them. She must have been a valid prophetess because the people sought her out. She was a woman of character.

NOTES FOR

HULDAH-A PROPHETESS

ANNA –A PRAYING WOMAN

Luke 2:36-37–And there was one Anna, a prophetess, the daughter of Phanuel, of the tribe of Aser; she was of a great age, and had lived with a husband seven years from her virginity; And she was a widow of about fourscore and four years, which departed not from the temple, but served God with fasting and prayers night and day.

Anna was serious about serving the Lord, even after she lost her husband. She prayed twenty-four hours a day. We do not know how long each prayer lasted, we just know she prayed all day long. She prayed without ceasing.

NOTES FOR

ANNA –A PRAYING WOMAN

THE WOMAN OF ZARAPHATH

1 Kings 17:7-16—Some time later the brook dried up because there had been no rain in the land. Then the word of the Lord came to him: "Go at once to Zarephath of Sidon and stay there. I have commanded a widow in that place to supply you with food." So he went to Zarephath. When he came to the town gate, a widow was there gathering sticks He called to her and asked, "Would you bring me a little water in a jar so I may have a drink?" As she was going to get it, he called, "And bring me, please, a piece of bread." As surely as the Lord your God lives," she replied, "I don't have any bread—only a handful of flour in

THE WOMAN OF ZARAPHATH

(CONTINUED

a jar and a little oil in a jug. I am gathering a few sticks to take home and make a meal for myself and my son that we may eat it–and die." Elijah said to her, Don't be afraid. Go home and do as you have said. But first make a small cake of bread for me, from what you have and bring it to me, and then make something for yourself and your son. For this is what the Lord, the God of Israel, says: the jar of flour will not be used up and the jug of oil will not run dry until the day the Lord gives rain on the land." She went away and did as Elijah had told her.

THE WOMAN OF ZARAPHATH

(CONTINUED)

For the jar of flour was not used up and the jug of oil did not run dry, in keeping with the word of the Lord spoken by Elijah. (NIV)

This widow was a woman of faith and obedience. At first she thought she and her son would die. She decided to listen to Elijah. She realized he was speaking what the Lord stated. She had enough faith to act on what he said. They ended up with plenty of food.

NOTES FOR

THE WOMAN OF ZARAPHATH

Scripture references:

(MSG) The Message, Eugene H. Peterson, Copyright 1993, 1994, 1995, 1996, 2000, 2001, 2002, NavPress Publishing Group

(NIV) Holy Bible, New International Version. Copyright 1973, 1978, 1984, International Bible Society.

(NKJV) The Holy Bible, New King James Version. Copyright 1982, Thomas Nelson, Inc.

(TLB) The Living Bible, Kenneth Taylor, Copyright 1974, Tyndale House Publishers, Inc.

The LORD is my light and the one who saves me.
   I fear no one.
The LORD protects my life;
   I am afraid of no one.
Evil people may try to destroy my body.
   My enemies and those who hate me attack me,
but they are overwhelmed and defeated.
If an army surrounds me,
   I will not be afraid.
If war breaks out,
   I will trust in the LORD.

LORD, teach me your ways,
   and guide me to do what is right
   because I have enemies.
Do not hand me over to my enemies,
   because they tell lies about me
   and say they will hurt me.

I truly believe
   I will live to see the LORD's goodness.
Wait for the LORD's help.
   Be strong and brave,
   and wait for the LORD's help.

—Psalm 27:1-3, 11-14

Introduction

This story takes place in Poland. Poland is a country in eastern Europe. Germany, Czechoslovakia, and Russia are on each side of Poland. At the time of this story, Germany was divided into West and East Germany.

Poland has often been ruled by other countries. During World War II, Poland was taken over by Nazi Germany. The Germans were cruel. They killed millions of Polish people.

After the war, in 1945, the Russians moved into Poland. They set up a Communist government. The Communists tried to control everyone. People who disagreed were punished. The Communists ruled Poland for 44 years.

However, most people didn't agree with Communism. They still wanted freedom. They trusted the Catholic church, not the government. And the church guided their thoughts and lives.

Around 1980, some things changed. The Communists began to soften. They let the Polish workers decide some things for themselves. But then the people wanted even more freedoms.

At the same time, the economy in Poland was a mess. There were not enough clothes, food, or medicine in the stores. There were not enough apartments to live in. Even if people had money, there was little to buy.

By 1981, the Polish people were still struggling for freedom. They were also struggling to find housing, food, and clothes.

Our story begins in 1981. It is based on a true story. Some things have been changed. But Ewa is a real person, and most of the events in this story really happened.

Chapter 1
Waiting in Line

October, 1981

Ewa tried to run, but her legs were too tired. "Hurry," she told herself. She had slept too long. It was 2:00 A.M., and she had told Zofia she would come at midnight. Her body felt stiff with sleep as she tried to run.

Soon Ewa got to the meat store. Many people were still there. They were waiting for meat in the middle of the night. Tomorrow the meat store would open again. Then, one by one, they would take turns buying meat. Some people had been waiting for two days!

Many people were sleeping. Some leaned against nearby buildings. Others brought chairs to sleep in.

Ewa felt cold as she looked around in the dark for Zofia. "Why didn't I take a blanket?" she thought. Then she saw her neighbor, Mrs. Bartowska.

"Hello, Mrs. Bartowska," Ewa said softly as she walked by. "Are you feeling all right? Don't worry. You are near the front of the line. Surely you will get meat tomorrow." Old Mrs. Bartowska nodded her head. She pulled her two blankets around her.

Ewa kept walking. There were people everywhere. At last Ewa saw Zofia. She was sitting in a chair close to another young woman. They were sleeping. One blanket covered them. The other woman's head rested on Zofia's shoulder.

"Zofia," Ewa said softly as she shook her friend's shoulder. "Zofia, wake up. You can go home now." Zofia tried to open her eyes.

"Ewa, what time is it? I must have fallen asleep." Zofia carefully pulled her arm out from under the sleeping woman's head. She stretched her arm. It was very stiff. Then she looked at her watch. "Ewa, it's after 2:00! Why are you so late?"

"Sorry, I slept too long. Go home. Go to sleep. I'll stay here four hours this time too. Come back at 6:00 or so." Ewa saw several people stirring. Some were watching her now.

Zofia shook her head. It was hard to think in the middle of the night. She slowly stood up. "What time do you teach?" Zofia whispered to Ewa.

Ewa and Zofia talked about their plans for the day. They would continue to take turns waiting. Zofia must be at her office job at 8:30 A.M. So Ewa would wait in line in the morning. Zofia would wait in the afternoon while Ewa taught at the music school.

Zofia stumbled towards her home. "I'll be back here at 6:00. Good night, Ewa," she said softly.

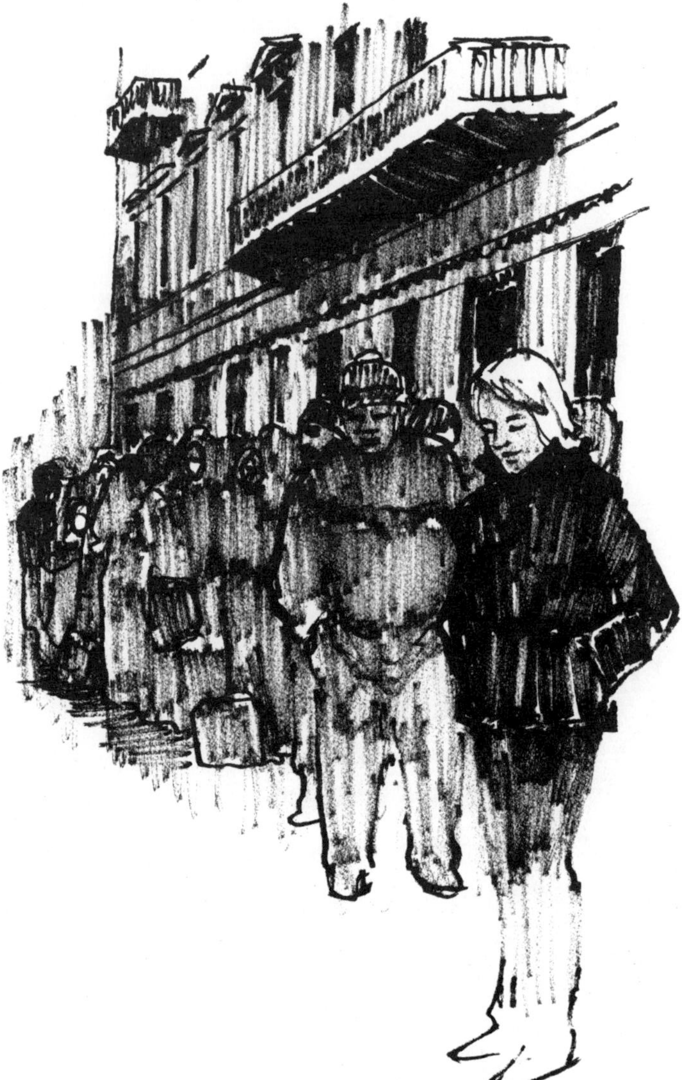

Chapter 2
Through the Night

Ewa sat down in Zofia's chair. She was wide awake now. She zipped up her jacket. She put some gloves on. She looked up at the stars. "Thank goodness it's not raining," she thought.

Then she looked at the people around her, and she felt angry. "Dear God," she thought, "what is happening to my country? There is not enough food to eat. How can we live like this? Soon it will be winter. Can we wait for meat outside in the snow?

"And where are our Communist leaders right now? They are sleeping in their warm beds! Their children's stomachs are filled with meat, milk, and cheese. While we wait in the cold for a small piece of meat. It's not fair!" Angry tears ran down Ewa's cheeks.

Ewa and her father had plenty of money. Ewa's father was retired. But every month he received a check from his old business. And Ewa had two jobs. She was a music and dance teacher during the day. She played the piano for a dance group at night.

But their money did not help them much. There was so little to buy. Stores all over Poland were almost empty. The stores would get some food and clothes to sell. But long lines of people were waiting to buy them.

Ewa moved her legs to warm them. "Nothing is worth this wait!" she thought angrily. "Two days and two nights is too long!"

Tomorrow would be the last day of October. After that it was too late to buy meat with her October coupons. She *must* get her meat tomorrow. If she didn't get meat tomorrow, her meat coupons would be worthless.

Ewa thought some more about tomorrow. All morning she would wait in line. Then in the afternoon she would teach piano lessons at the music school. Tomorrow she had lessons all afternoon. In the evening she would play the piano for a dance group. How could she do all this with so little sleep?

Most people had families to help wait in lines. But not Ewa. Her father walked stiffly with crutches. Once he was knocked over in a food line. Now he refused to wait in one.

Ewa's brother and his wife lived in another city. Her mother had died two years ago. Every day Ewa missed her. Every night as she lay in bed she felt the same sadness. Tears started to roll down Ewa's cheeks.

"Oh, Mama," she thought now, "life is so hard without you. . . . There is so much I want to tell you. . . . I need you. . . ."

Ewa shook herself. Things would seem happier in the morning. Everything always seemed sad in the dark of night.

"Ewa, wake up! It's 6 o'clock." Ewa jerked awake. She was cold and stiff all over. And it was still dark. But there was Zofia, ready to take Ewa's place. Ewa stood up slowly. If she hurried home, she could sleep a little while in her warm bed.

"Hurry, Ewa," Zofia said. "Go home now. But be back at 8:00. And don't oversleep this time!" she added with a smile.

Ewa stumbled toward the apartment she shared with her father. "All this for a little meat," she thought.

Chapter 3
The Waiting Ends

All day, Ewa and Zofia took turns waiting for meat. Slowly the line moved forward. While Zofia worked, Ewa waited. Then Zofia came back to wait, and Ewa hurried to her teaching.

Finally it was 4:30 P.M. Ewa finished her last piano lesson. She was tired. But it was her turn to wait in line.

With heavy steps she walked towards the meat store. Now Zofia could go rest. But before Ewa got to the line, Zofia met her.

"Ewa," she said, "the line is finished. You can go home now."

"Oh, Zofia, thank goodness! I'm so tired. So what kind of meat did you get? Where is it? Did you take it home? Thanks for helping me!" Ewa was excited.

"Sorry," said Zofia sadly. "There is no meat. It was gone before I got into the store. All gone. The shopkeeper sent us home. No more meat until November."

Chapter 4
Time to Teach Again

January, 1982

Ewa put her head down as she walked home. The wind blew hard. Snowflakes stung her eyes. It was turning dark. Ewa put her collar up and pulled her scarf across her face.

A few blocks later she entered her apartment building. She hurried down the hall. With stiff fingers she unlocked the door. She could smell meat cooking. "That smell is not coming from my apartment," she thought. Tiredly she walked inside.

"Papa, I'm home," Ewa called. She hung up her coat. She set her wet boots on a small piece of rug and pushed an old blanket against the door. It kept the cold air from coming under the door.

"Papa, I'm home," she called again. She walked into the living room. The apartment felt cozy and warm. She could smell food cooking as she walked to the kitchen.

"Hi, Papa," she said. "I got some butter this afternoon." Reaching into her bag, she added, "Look, I bought soap too. But there was no meat today."

Her father stood by the stove. He was leaning on a crutch and stirring a pot of potato soup. A warm loaf of bread was on the table. "The meat is not important," he said. "Sit down, Ewa. You look tired."

On the table was a letter for Ewa. "This letter came today," her father said. "It's from your school."

"I know what this is," said Ewa as she opened it. "My school will begin next week. In town, everybody is talking about it. The

Communists have said that all schools will open again next week."

Ewa's father watched her unfold the letter. She looked angry. There was a frown on her face. "What's wrong, Ewa?" her father asked. "Aren't you happy? Don't you want to teach again?"

"Why should I be happy?" Ewa's words were hard and angry. "You know how the director at school treats me. He doesn't like me because I won't join the Communist Party. He never says my teaching is good. He watches me with a frown on his face.

"And now Poland is in a state of war. I think things will get worse for me at school. The director will act like nothing has happened. He will greet us teachers with a smile. But I know him. He will watch me even more now. I will have to be very, very careful.

"No, Papa, I'm not happy that school is beginning. I am afraid to go back next week."

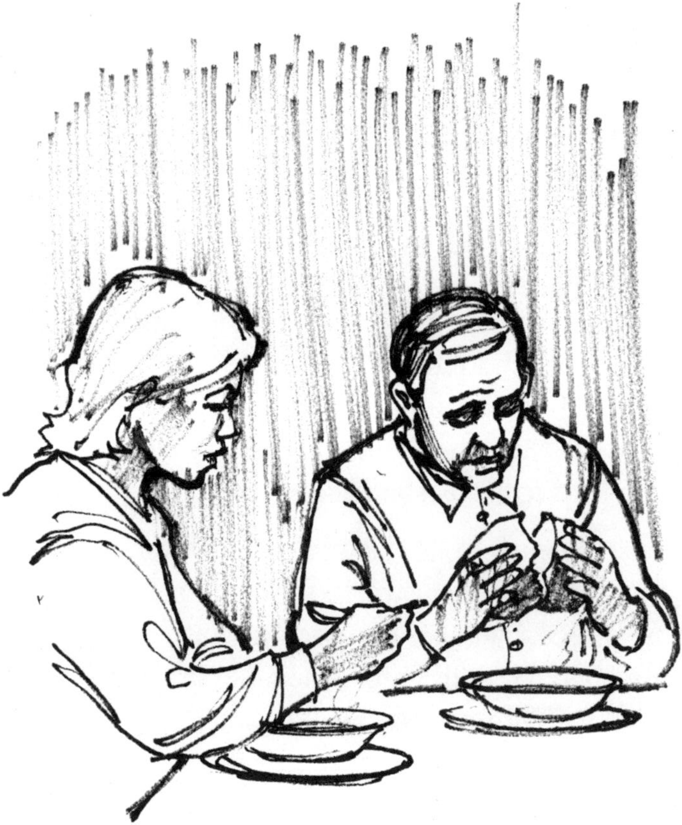

Chapter 5
State of War

Ewa's father put two bowls of soup on the table. He sat down by his daughter. What should he say to her? These were very dark days for the Polish people. Last month the Communists had put Poland in a state of war.

That meant that the Communists had taken every freedom away. They cut all telephone lines. Every newspaper and news program had been taken over by Communists. People were not allowed to leave their towns. They could not gather in groups. All schools were closed.

Now there were soldiers everywhere. And the Communists had arrested thousands of Polish leaders. Many of the leaders who wanted more freedoms for Poland were now in jail.

Before the state of war, life was hard. People suffered because there was not enough food. They complained about the long lines. But there was hope because the Communists were becoming kinder. Now that hope was gone too.

Ewa and her father ate in silence. Papa watched as Ewa cut a piece of bread. He was proud of his daughter. Young people like Ewa were the hope for Poland. They would not let their spirits be broken by Communism.

Papa remembered when he was young. At that time the Germans controlled Poland. It was during World War II. Life was much worse then. People all over Poland were starving. And the Germans killed anyone who disobeyed them.

Ewa's father remembered living in the forest. A large group of Polish men were hiding there. They attacked the Germans whenever they could. Finally he was caught. He was put in prison. He could not think about those terrible days in prison.

But he, like Ewa, had not let his spirit be broken. He never lost hope. He always knew his country would be free again. Now he looked at Ewa.

"Ewa," he said gently. "Don't lose hope. The Communists will soften again. You are a wonderful teacher. Teach as you always have. Your students and their parents really like your teaching, right? Keep doing good work, and don't worry about the director."

Ewa shook her head slowly. "It's not that easy, Papa. Remember last summer? Remember when I signed papers to teach for this school year? At that time the director asked me to join the Communist Party."

"Yes, of course, Ewa," said her father. "You told him you wanted to think about it. You told him you were not ready to join the party. Well, you must tell him the same thing next summer."

"Yes, Papa, I will." Ewa sighed. "But they might give my job to someone else. Even if I keep the job, I will never advance. I will never get a better job. The important jobs will go to Communists. I am almost 24 years old. What is my future?"

Ewa stood up. She sang a Communist song all Polish children must learn. Loudly she sang, "Get up! Get up! Everyone, lift your heads high. If we stand together, we will have a better life. Days of victory are coming for us."

Then she dropped back into her chair. "What a joke. Days of victory for who? Not me! I'm so tired of it all. Tired of being careful of every word I say. Tired of lazy Communists getting better jobs than me. Why, some Communist teachers at school can't even sing on tune! Oh, Papa, what am I going to do?"

Chapter 6
Away from Home

March, 1982

Ewa looked out of the train window. She was happy to be leaving her town, Chelmno, for the weekend. The sky was blue and the sun was bright. It was a great day!

Just like Papa said, the Communists were softening. They were becoming kinder. Now they allowed people to travel outside their towns. So Ewa was going to visit Gdansk. This city was north of Chelmno on the Baltic Sea. Here, her brother Adam lived with his wife,

Grazyna. Ewa was excited to leave her small town and go to the big city.

But she was mostly excited to see Adam and Grazyna. They had not come to Chelmno for Christmas. Because of the state of war, they could not leave Gdansk. Ewa and her father missed them very much. But the worst part was not seeing baby Mariusz.

Ewa had bought the baby a beautiful sweater for Christmas. That was three months ago. Now Ewa was afraid the sweater might be too small for him. But she had brought it along anyway. "Let's see," she thought, "Mariusz was five months at Christmas. He must be eight months now."

Ewa wished Papa could have come too. But his legs were too stiff and sore. She would ask Adam and Grazyna to visit Papa in Chelmno soon.

Chapter 7
A Visit with Family

By early afternoon, Ewa was in Gdansk. She ran to her brother's apartment. She pounded on their door. "Adam! Grazyna! I'm here," she called eagerly.

"Wait, Ewa, just a second," Ewa listened to Grazyna's voice on the other side of the door. "Let me open the lock," she said. "Shhh . . . now, don't cry . . . here's your aunt." The door opened.

Ewa and Grazyna kissed each other happily. Then Ewa took the baby from

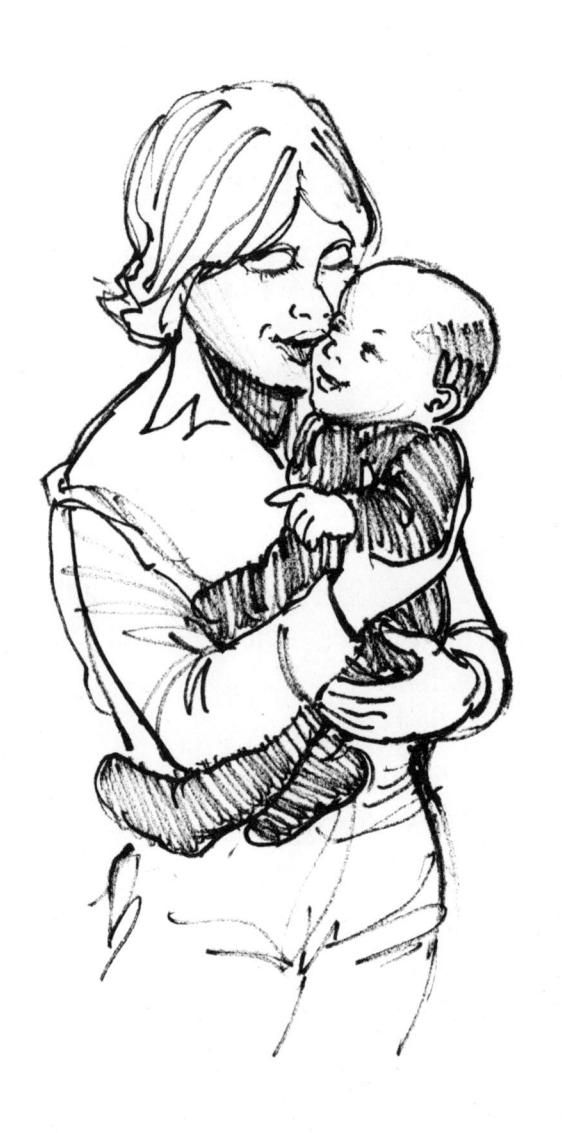

Grazyna's arms. She kissed his chubby cheeks over and over.

"Oh, Mariusz . . . my little one, you've grown so much. You're such a big boy! Oh, Grazyna, he's beautiful," Ewa said softly. Tears ran down her cheeks. Then she added, "Mariusz, just wait. My bags are full of good things for you!"

The rest of the day passed quickly. Ewa played with little Mariusz. And she talked and talked with Adam and Grazyna. Friends would stop by and join their talk for a while.

They talked about what was happening in Poland. The Communists were not so kind to the people in Gdansk. This large city had many leaders who demanded freedom. Now most of them were in prison.

Many workers in Gdansk did not obey the new Communist rules. So army tanks had come to these places. Polish soldiers shot at Polish workers.

Hard anger showed in Adam's face as he talked. "What is happening to our country? Polish people shooting Polish people?" he asked. "But we must never stop working for change. The Communists can't scare us! Already people are secretly writing newspapers to tell the truth."

Ewa sat quietly. Her brother's courage scared her. But she was proud of him. "Ewa, you still wear your pin," Adam said. "That's good. But be careful here in Gdansk. Be sure the police don't see it."

Before the state of war, people all over Poland wore special pins. These pins showed they did not like Communist rule. But now it was illegal to wear them.

Before Ewa could answer, Grazyna called from the bedroom. "Come, Ewa, little Mariusz is ready for bed. Do you want to hold him first? I'll go make us something to eat."

Chapter 8
A Beautiful Sunday

Sunday morning, Ewa and Adam went to church. Grazyna stayed home with the baby. As they entered, they saw that the church was nearly full.

Ewa felt happy when she saw all the people. The Polish people never stopped believing in God. If anything, their love of God was stronger than before.

Ewa knelt to pray. "Oh, God," she prayed silently, "help your people. We just want to be free to make decisions for ourselves. How long can we wait? Oh, God, how long must we wait?" Tears came to her eyes.

She prayed, "Lord Jesus, I don't know about my life. What is going to happen to me? What about my music? Please help me know what to do."

After church, Ewa and Adam walked out by the sea. Soon it would be time for Ewa to take the train back to Chelmno.

The sky was blue with bright, white clouds. It was very warm for March. The brother and sister walked quickly. The soft spring air put energy in their steps.

They talked quickly too. There was so much to say and so little time. Ewa told Adam about the director at her school. She told him about her students. But there was something else she needed to say.

"Adam, do you know the dance group that I practice with?" she began.

"Sure," Adam said. "You play the piano for them, right?"

"Right. Well, they want me to be their director. We're trying to put their dance acts with the music of a folk band. There are 33 of us in all—the band, the dancers, and me."

"Whew!" said Adam. "That sounds like hard work. Do you like it?"

Ewa laughed. "Well, it's not easy. It's hard to keep the dances and the music moving at the same time. The hardest part is when the music stops. Then everyone has a different idea about everything. You should hear us argue! But it's fun. I like it."

Adam laughed too. "I would like to see you at work. How can you keep 33 people from fighting with each other? Remember when we were kids? You started a fight with me every time we were playing."

Ewa punched Adam's shoulder. "*I* started those fights?" she laughed. "No, Adam, *you* liked to fight. You still do."

Then Ewa became serious. "Adam, there is something else. I need to tell you something else. There is a rumor. A few of the dancers have been talking about it. Now remember, it's just a rumor. Our group may be asked to perform . . . in the Netherlands."

Adam whistled softly. "In the Netherlands? What a chance for you! It's so hard to get outside of Poland. No one can get a visa to go anywhere."

"It's just a rumor, Adam," Ewa said. Then she spoke very quickly. "But I can't stop thinking about it. If we really go, do you think I should stay there? I mean should I defect in the Netherlands? Adam, there is no future for me in Poland!"

Chapter 9
Adam's Story

Ewa's heart pounded. She had not said these things to anyone else. Would she dare to stay in the Netherlands? Could she leave Poland? Where would she live? What would she do? It was just an idea in her mind. What would Adam say about it?

Adam looked at his younger sister. For a minute he didn't say anything. "Ewa, I've never told you . . . but I planned to defect a few years ago. It must have been 1978. Remember when I took that trip to West Germany?"

Ewa nodded her head and waited. Adam said, "I wasn't going to come back to Poland. I wanted a better life. I had everything planned.

"But before I left for West Germany, I came home. I wanted to say goodbye to you all. And remember? Mama was already sick with cancer."

Oh, yes, with great pain Ewa remembered. "Well," Adam said, "Mama was lying on the couch. I held her hands and kissed her goodbye. And do you know what she said to me? She said, 'Adam, please come back. Come back home after your trip.'"

Adam waited for a minute. "I never told Mama that I wanted to defect, to leave Poland. I never told any of you. But Mama knew. She just knew."

Ewa and Adam walked quietly for a moment. There were tears in Adam's eyes. "So I came back. I had to come back to Mama."

"But Mama died the next year," Ewa said quietly.

"Oh, I know," said Adam. "But I lost my chance. How could I get another visa to West

Germany? And Grazyna and I were falling in love . . . and now there is Mariusz. . . . Ewa, I have no plans to go anymore. But *you*, my little sister?"

Adam was only two years older than Ewa. But often he still treated her like a child.

Ewa answered, "Remember, the trip is just a rumor, Adam. Even if we do go . . . well, I don't think I could defect. How could I leave Papa? He can't stand in line with his crutches. He needs me to take care of him."

"Ewa," said Adam quickly. "He's my father too. If you leave Poland, Grazyna and I will take care of him. Remember how Grazyna helped when Mama was so sick? Of course we will take care of him."

"But you've been away for so long now," Ewa said. She waited, still thinking about it. Then she added, "And Papa wouldn't like it at all. He'd think I was deserting my homeland if I left."

"Ewa," Adam spoke firmly. "If you get the chance, if you want to defect . . . then *go*. Papa is 68. He has lived his life. Only you can decide about your own life."

For a few moments they walked in silence. Then they talked about other things. At last it was time to say goodbye. Adam would go home. Ewa needed to walk a few blocks to the train station. They kissed each other. "Adam, visit us soon," Ewa called as she ran toward the train station.

Chapter 10

A Beautiful Sunday Ruined

Ewa ran faster. It was getting late. She must get home tonight. As she ran, she thought about her brother. She wished he, Grazyna, and baby Mariusz lived closer to Chelmno!

Suddenly Ewa saw a policeman coming. She slowed down. She looked straight ahead. "You! You! Miss! Stop right now." The policeman was talking to her.

"Oh, no," Ewa thought, "I don't need this now." She stopped.

"Show me your ID card, Miss," the policeman said. Since the state of war, everyone had to carry an ID card. It gave their name, age, address, and job. Ewa pulled her card out of her purse.

Slowly the policeman looked it over. He asked her some questions. What was she doing in Gdansk? Where was she going? Ewa answered politely. Then he looked right at the pin that Ewa wore everywhere.

A sick feeling came over Ewa. The sunshine and fast walking had made her warm. She had taken off her coat. She forgot about the pin on her sweater. The policeman pointed to the pin. "What is this?" he asked.

"It's a pin," Ewa said. She tried to make her voice sound calm. But her heart was pounding wildly. "I like to wear it with this sweater."

Smack! Ewa fell backwards as the policeman slapped her face. Anger and pain filled her heart. But her face still looked calm. "Take it off," the policeman ordered. "You are lucky today. I should report you to the authorities. But if you do as I say, maybe I won't."

"Yes, sir," Ewa said quietly. She took the pin off and put it in her purse.

"No! Throw that thing away. Throw it away. Now!" The policeman's voice was very stern. Ewa pulled her pin out of her purse. She tossed it into the bushes. The policeman left with an angry frown on his face.

Ewa began to walk toward the train station. She felt her burning cheek. Tears filled her eyes. "What can I do? How can I live in this country? Oh, Jesus, help me," she sobbed.

Then she looked back at the policeman. He was turning down another street. Quickly Ewa ran back. Quickly she looked in the bushes. There was the pin lying in the dirt. She picked it up, dropped it into her purse, and ran toward the train station.

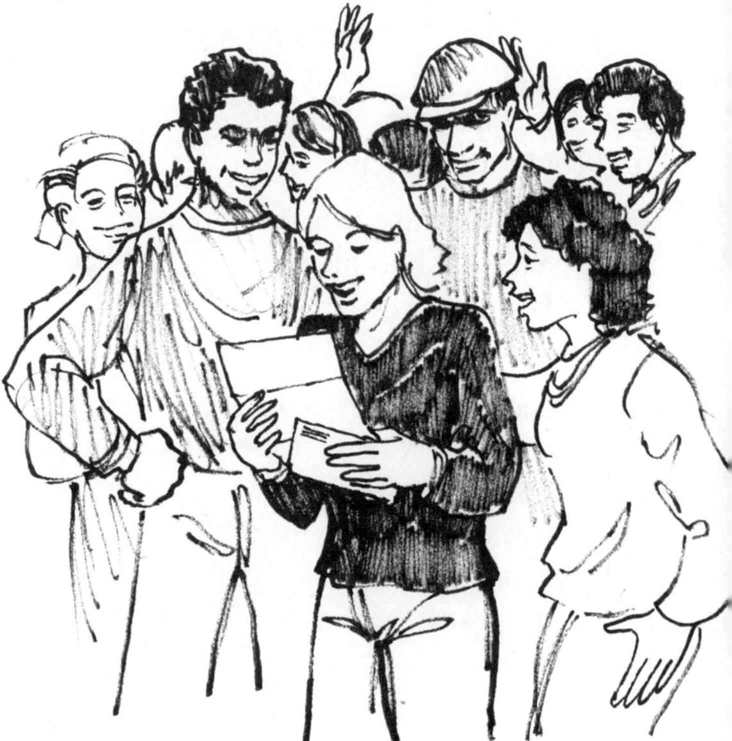

Chapter 11
An Invitation

May-June, 1982

Ewa waited at the piano for the others to arrive. She felt important. It was almost 7:45 P.M. Their practice was supposed to begin at 7:00 P.M. Most of the dancers and band members were still outside talking. They were enjoying the warm evening. Several of the girl dancers had not come yet.

Ewa sighed. She had played through the music twice already. She was ready to begin. She had plans to meet Zofia and two men after the practice. So she did not want to practice late tonight.

Suddenly the dancers hurried into the room. Everyone was there. "Come on, let's start," Ewa said. "I've got plans for later tonight."

"Ewa," said Kasia, one of the women dancers. "I'm sorry we are late. But we have a good reason. Read this letter." And she gave Ewa a letter.

Ewa looked at the envelope. It was from the Netherlands. She opened it slowly. Her heart pounded. Could it be? Slowly she read the letter. Then she looked up. Everyone in the group was watching her.

"Kasia, you were right!" she said. "They have invited us to perform in Lelystad. In the Netherlands. It's wonderful. . . . I just can't believe it is true!"

Some of the dancers nearby exploded with excitement. They hugged each other and yelled out cheers. Others danced around the room with joy.

"Wait a minute," said one of the male dancers. "Now just a minute. Will someone explain to *me* what is going on? Why would anyone ask us to perform in Lelystad? What's going on?"

Kasia waited a moment. When it was quieter, she said, "I'll explain. If you'll listen, I'll explain. Some of you know about my uncle in Lelystad. But some of you don't. So just listen a minute, OK?"

Kasia sat down on a chair. Everyone quieted down. Some sat on chairs, others on the floor.

Kasia began her story. "My uncle moved from Chelmno to Lelystad five years ago. He got a job in a large business there. He's an accountant, I think. Something like that. Well, anyway, he told some of the people at his business about Poland . . . and about us here in Chelmno.

"He told them about our empty stores. He told how we waited in terrible lines. He said there was not enough food or clothes for us. Well, I think the people in Lelystad were shocked. They didn't know how bad it was here. And so the business decided to help.

"Other people from Lelystad heard the story. They wanted to help the people of Chelmno too. So the town got many, many things for us—food, soap, clothes, shoes, even a few wheelchairs. A whole truckload of things for us!

"They took the things to a couple of churches in Chelmno last fall. The priests gave everything to people in need. Believe me, there were a lot of people who needed that stuff."

Kasia continued, "Mother wrote a letter to my uncle. She said that we were very, very thankful. She said the people of Chelmno wanted to thank the people of Lelystad. She hoped that our dance group could perform there. That's how we could thank them."

Kasia clapped her hands. "This," she said, "is the letter that invites us to perform in Lelystad!" Everyone in the room started clapping and dancing.

"We're going to the Netherlands!" called out one happy young man.

"Wait a minute," said Ewa. "Wait a minute. Kasia, is there more to your story? Did your mother show this letter to the authorities? Have they agreed to let us go?" Ewa felt her heart beat with excitement. Could it be? Would the authorities agree?

"That is why I'm late." Kasia smiled. "Mother and I went to ask an official. We waited more than four hours to see him."

"And?" said another dancer. "And he agreed?"

"Well," said Kasia, "we have to go back in two weeks. Then they will give us the final answer. But I'm quite sure they will let us go. The official was very nice. He knows mother and my uncle.

"In fact, I think he got some of the clothes from Lelystad. Anyway, he thinks dancing in Lelystad is a good idea. He said there should be no problem."

Everyone cheered and talked at the same time. It was hard to practice! At last Ewa said, "Let's go home. If we do go on this trip, we will have to practice very hard. But tonight let's just be happy."

Ewa walked home slowly. Later she would meet Zofia and the men. But for now, Ewa wanted to think. She thought about her talk with Adam. Now the thought of leaving Poland filled her with fear and pain.

"Oh, God," she prayed, "thank you for this chance to visit the Netherlands. May we dance well!" And she added, "And thank you for my family, my friends, and my jobs here in Poland."

Chapter 12
Tomasz

It was official! The dance group was going to the Netherlands. Everyone had just six weeks to get ready. They must practice every evening.

Ewa wanted everything to be perfect—the dancing and the music. She wanted the Dutch people to love Polish folk music. And to see how good a Polish folk dance group could be.

But there were problems. One of the violinists became very ill. Then two male dancers were forced to join the Polish army. Ewa found a new violinist and one new dancer. But they still needed one more male dancer.

Ewa hurried home from teaching one day. As she walked, she heard someone call her name. "Ewa . . . wait a minute, Ewa!" Ewa saw Tomasz behind her. Tomasz was Zofia's friend.

"Tomasz, how are you?" Ewa stopped and waited for him. "Zofia said you wanted to talk to me. What's up?"

Tomasz ran to catch up with Ewa. He was breathing hard. "So, Ewa, how are you doing? How is your dance group? I hear you are leaving our fair homeland, Poland. I hear you are spending two weeks in the Netherlands. Lucky girl."

Ewa laughed. "Believe me, Tomasz, we are working hard for it. The trip will be nice. But for now, it's only hard work and more hard work."

"Listen, Ewa," Tomasz said, "Zofia said you need another dancer."

"Right," Ewa answered, "and we had better find one soon. Otherwise we're going to be in trouble!"

"Well, what about me?" Tomasz asked. "I'd like to join you."

"*You,* Tomasz?" Ewa looked surprised. She didn't know that Tomasz danced. He didn't seem like a dancer. Why would he want to join their dance group?

Tomasz knew what Ewa was thinking. "You know, Ewa, I did dance a little in school. And you could help me," he said. "Besides I'm a pretty good athlete. I'll learn fast!" Tomasz stopped talking as they came to Ewa's apartment.

"Come on in," Ewa said, "let's talk about it with a cup of tea."

For almost an hour Ewa and Tomasz talked about the dance group. Ewa's father poured cups of hot tea and listened. Finally it was decided. If the rest of the group agreed, Tomasz could join. Ewa agreed to teach him the dances every night before the practices.

Chapter 13
Too Many Questions

Many hours later that night, Ewa lay in bed awake. The music of the evening's practice filled her mind. And she couldn't stop thinking about Tomasz. The others had agreed to let him join. But Tomasz couldn't dance. At least not yet...

Ewa sighed. How could she teach him? She already had too much to do. Her teaching job, playing with the dance group, and now teaching Tomasz! There was also time for standing in line for food, time for her father, time for her friends....

53

Ewa rolled, then rolled over again. Why had Tomasz joined the dance group? It must be for the Lelystad trip. What other reason could there be? Why else would he want to join? He must want to leave Poland and stay in the West.

But learning the dances would be hard work! It would take so much of his time! Was there a reason he had to leave Poland *now?* He had a good job. Ewa sighed.

Ewa's thoughts turned back to herself. Several weeks had passed since Kasia brought the letter to practice. Since that day, Ewa could think of nothing but leaving. Should she leave Poland? Should she stay in the Netherlands?

Some days she was sure she must leave. Like the day last week when she had trouble at school. She had let an older girl play a popular song from the West. The Communist director had heard about it.

So at the next teachers' meeting he talked about the West. Over and over he talked about their music. He blamed their music for the moral problems of the West. He hadn't said

Ewa's name. But he looked right at her while he was talking.

But then Ewa would come home to Papa. She watched him pull himself along with his crutches. She saw how lonely he was without Mama. Then she knew she must stay.

"Oh, God," she prayed as she felt sleep finally coming. "I can't see what I should do. Guide me. Show me the best way."

Chapter 14
A Plan

Only two weeks until the trip! The group would not practice that Tuesday evening. Everyone was too busy and too tired. Besides, the dances were looking very good.

That gave Ewa an extra evening to work with Tomasz. Dancing was not easy for him. Ewa sighed. She thought about the way Tomasz moved. He was so stiff. He couldn't flow with the music. He really needed the extra practice.

Tomasz was going to come to her house. Ewa listened to music by Chopin while she waited. She sat back and closed her eyes. She let the music of the Polish composer sweep over her. She felt very tired.

But she couldn't stop her tired mind. It kept going back to the trip. If she defected, where would she stay? How could she find a job? Was there anyone to help her? She needed a plan!

She wanted to talk with Adam again. She couldn't talk with anyone here in Chelmno. What if a Communist official heard that someone planned to defect? There would be no trip. It would be canceled right away.

And what if Papa got the idea Ewa might defect? That would be worse. Just one sad look from Papa, and Ewa could not do it. Just as Mama's gentle words brought Adam home many years ago.

Ewa had no relatives in the West. But she had a friend from music school who had left Poland. Eliza lived in West Germany. Ewa had her address. But it would be so much easier to escape in the Netherlands. How could Ewa contact Eliza in Germany? Ewa sighed.

Ewa had a plan. She would write to Eliza. As soon as they got to Lelystad she would mail the letter. She would ask Eliza to call her. By then Ewa would know what to do. She could ask Eliza for help.

But what if Eliza had moved? Or what if she didn't call Ewa in Lelystad? Ewa sighed. It wasn't a very good plan. But it was something.

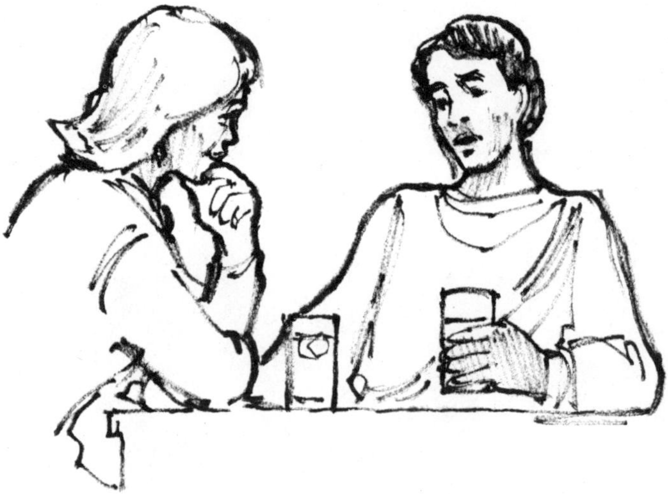

Chapter 15
A Shared Secret

Ewa and Tomasz practiced and practiced. Finally Tomasz said, "Enough, Ewa! My legs are tired. I'm tired all over! What do you think?"

Ewa laughed. "You're doing better, Tomasz. Your dancing is much better. Try to practice a little at home. Now, let's get something cold to drink before you go."

Papa was already in bed. So Ewa and Tomasz went quietly to the kitchen. As they drank, they talked about the trip to Lelystad. Ewa wanted to ask Tomasz her question. She must do it now. They might never be alone like this again.

Ewa took a deep breath. "Tomasz, you don't plan to come back, do you? You are going to defect in the Netherlands," she said.

Tomasz was quiet for a moment. His face turned red. He stared at Ewa. "You're crazy, Ewa. Why would I do that? I've got my job and family here."

Ewa couldn't stop. "But dancing, Tomasz. You dancing? Why are you going through all this pain? Learning these dances is hard, hard work. You wouldn't do it for a quick visit to the Netherlands. Tomasz, you can trust me. Honestly."

The room was quiet. Then Ewa whispered, "I'm thinking about it too. I might defect too." There! She had said it. She had finally told someone.

Tomasz stared at Ewa. He wanted to trust her. Why would she want to hurt him? Did he dare tell her? Could this be a trick?

Again the room was quiet. At last Tomasz spoke. "Yes, Ewa, I hope to defect in Lelystad.

I can't stay in Poland much longer. If I do, I'll be forced to join the army. I hope to stay with relatives in West Germany."

Ewa's heart pounded. She looked up at Tomasz. So that was it! The Communists were going to force him to join the army. That was why he needed to defect right away.

Ewa must trust Tomasz. At once she was eager to tell him her plans. She needed to talk to someone about defecting. "I have a friend, Eliza, in West Germany. I may stay with her. But I may come back to Poland. I am not sure what to do."

"Ewa, let's do it together!" Thomasz was excited. "Let's run together. If you need to, you can stay with my relatives. At least until you find something else. Anyway we need more than one plan. We don't know what will happen. We can't be sure when or where we will be able to escape."

Ewa and Tomasz whispered for a long time. They would wait until the dance group was finished performing. They would need to get foreign money. And they agreed that one thing was the most important. They *must not* tell anyone else about their plans.

Chapter 16
Last Day in Chelmno

It was a cool day for the end of June. The wind blew. Ewa looked at the clouds. She hoped it wouldn't rain before she got home. She pulled on her sweater.

Ewa carried a bunch of red roses. She was bringing them to her mother's grave. She walked quickly until she got to the grave. She looked around. She was glad no one else was near her.

She knelt down with the flowers. Her tears began as she put the flowers on Mama's grave.

"Oh, Mama, Mama," Ewa cried. For a few minutes she couldn't say more.

"I'm sorry I haven't come for a few days. The last days of school were so busy. And Papa left for the lake on Monday. . . . And Mama, I leave for Lelystad tomorrow. Tomorrow morning!" Again Ewa sobbed, this time even harder.

"Papa never guessed. He didn't guess that I might defect. If you were here, you would know, Mama. Women know these things better than men. . . .

"I've told you so many times already. You know I love Papa. But there is no future for me here. There is only trouble for me at the school. But if I don't teach what will I do?

"Mama, I'm leaving it in God's hands. If he shows me a way to run in Lelystad, I won't be back. But if there is no way, then that is God's will. I will be back here in two weeks.

"And if I don't come back, Mama . . . if I don't come back, I know you will still be near me.

"Oh, Mama, I'm so scared. I'm so very scared!" Again Ewa sobbed quietly. She didn't feel the rain begin.

Ewa cried into her arms for ten minutes. The sky grew black, the wind blew hard. The rain came in small drops. Then Ewa felt a hand on her shoulder.

She looked up. There stood an old woman. The woman looked at her with soft, kind eyes. "There, there, child," she said. "May God bless you. Believe in him. He will be with you in your time of need." Then the woman walked slowly away.

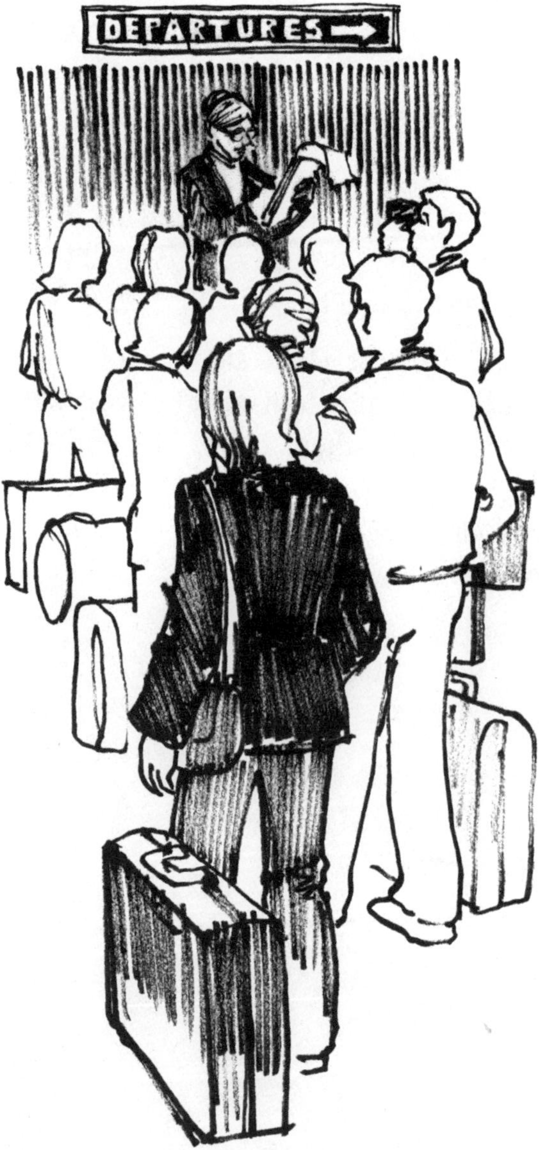
DEPARTURES

Chapter 17
Mrs. Ola

July, 1982

Ewa got to the bus station at 9 A.M. The dance group was to leave later in the morning. They planned to stay that night in East Germany and get to Lelystad the next day.

Many of the group were already there. Ewa greeted each person warmly. "Good morning, Rysiu!" "Kasia, you look so nice this morning!" But where was Tomasz? Ewa looked all around for him. She hoped he wouldn't be late this time.

Just then a Communist official walked in. He was with a group of eight Communist party members. They were older men and women. Most had gray hair. They would go with the dance group to the Netherlands. They would be "chaperons" for the group.

Everyone knew what the chaperons' job was. These Communists would watch the dancers and band players closely. No one must stay in the Netherlands. No one must defect. The chaperons would make sure that *everyone* returned to Poland.

Ewa looked closely at the chaperons. One looked older than Papa. How careful would they be? How closely would they watch her?

Just then Tomasz came running up. Ewa greeted him. Now she could relax. Everybody was here. All 33 of them, dancers, band members, and herself.

One of the officials stepped onto a platform. He ordered everyone to be quiet. He welcomed the dance group. He praised their fine musical talent. He said they were the pride of Poland. He knew they would perform well in Lelystad.

He talked on and on. He told the group how lucky they were. Not many Polish young people were asked to perform abroad. Again he said they would bring honor to Poland.

Ewa looked at the ground. Too much talk! The Communists always talked like this. She just wanted to get going.

Next the official talked about the eight chaperons. They would go with the group. The woman in charge was Mrs. Ola. Now it was Mrs. Ola's turn to talk. She had a list with the names of each dancer and band member. Slowly she read the names. She read six names. Then she named the chaperon who was going to be watching them.

She read names until everyone in the group had a chaperon. Everyone but Ewa. Ewa felt sick. Were they going to keep her here? Wasn't she going to go?

Finally Mrs. Ola read Ewa's name. Then she looked up. "I will be staying with Ewa," she said. "Now please line up with your bags. We are ready to pack and get on the bus."

Ewa stood there for a moment. She picked up her bag and walked slowly to the bus. Why was Mrs. Ola her chaperon? Why wasn't she in a group with five other dancers? The officials must be worried about her. But why?

Because she had no children or husband to come back for? Because her family had money? Because she was educated? Because the director at school said Ewa did not like Communism? Ewa shook her head slowly. This defecting was not going to be easy.

Chapter 18
Never Alone

The bus got to Lelystad the next afternoon. Everyone was put into a small group. Each small group went to the home of a different Dutch family. Everyone would stay with these families for the two weeks in Lelystad. Ewa and Mrs. Ola went to the home of a young Dutch family.

Ewa really enjoyed the family. They couldn't speak Polish. Ewa couldn't speak Dutch. But she knew a few words of English. So they tried to talk to each other in English. The young woman listened closely to Ewa.

Then she spoke slowly so Ewa could understand her.

The Dutch family lived in a small apartment. It was clean and cozy. Fresh flowers were on every table. The family made wonderful meals for Ewa and Mrs. Ola. It had been a long time since Ewa had enjoyed so much good food.

Every day the dance group gave a performance. They performed in many towns. But in their free time, everyone enjoyed the shops. Ewa had never left Communist Europe before. So the shops amazed her.

There was so much of everything. Every kind of food, pastry, and drink was here. And no one had to wait in lines. Ewa loved the clothes! The Dutch people dressed with so much style.

The group from Poland brought money with them. But what should they buy? Where should they start? There was too much to choose from.

Ewa bought three bananas. They looked wonderful. And they tasted so sweet. But she did not let herself spend more. If she escaped, she would need all her money.

Ewa was happy to be in the Netherlands. But Mrs. Ola spoiled Ewa's joy. Everywhere Ewa went, Mrs. Ola was there. They even slept in the same room. Mrs. Ola was right there at each performance. Mrs. Ola shopped with Ewa. And when Ewa went to the cafe with her friends, so did Mrs. Ola.

One night, Mrs. Ola and Ewa were lying in bed. Ewa turned off the light. Mrs. Ola said, "Ewa, I wonder about you. You surprise me."

"Oh no," thought Ewa, "now what?"

Mrs. Ola said, "Everyone is buying many things. They buy food, clothes, and gifts for their families. You have bought only three bananas. Why is that? I know you have money."

Ewa was ready to answer Mrs. Ola's question. She had planned her answer. "Well," she said with a yawn, "have you seen what everyone is buying? Many small things. Pastries and sweets. A sweater or a shirt. Maybe some perfume.

"All these things will soon be eaten or forgotten in Poland. I'm going to use my money for something of value. I want to buy a leather coat. A coat I will be proud of for many years."

"Oh," said Mrs. Ola, "a leather coat? Hmm . . . they are expensive. Well, we don't have much time left. You'll have to buy one soon."

Chapter 19
A Strange Phone Call

The next day Ewa was resting in her room. It was late afternoon. The dance group would perform in three hours. "Ewa, are you awake?" It was Mrs. Ola's voice again. She was outside the bedroom door.

Ewa tried not to sound angry. "Yes, I'm awake. Do you need something?" Ewa wished Mrs. Ola would just go away for a while.

"There is a phone call for you. A woman named Eliza. She's calling from West Germany. Shall I tell her to call back another time?" Mrs. Ola asked.

Ewa's heart pounded. It was Eliza . . . finally! Ewa had been waiting so long for this call. "No, it's an old friend. I'd like to talk to her," said Ewa. She jumped out of bed.

Mrs. Ola followed Ewa to the phone. She sat down in a chair. Ewa felt trapped. How could she talk to Eliza with Mrs. Ola there? She needed to find out if Eliza could help her. But Mrs. Ola was spoiling her chance.

Ewa picked up the phone. "Hello, Eliza," she said, "I'm so glad you called!" And for a few minutes the women shared the news of their lives. They talked about their families and their jobs.

At last Eliza asked, "Ewa, I got your letter. What's happening? Do you still want to defect? Do you want to come here to West Germany?"

Ewa's heart beat harder. She looked over at Mrs. Ola. Then she said to Eliza, "I'm looking for a leather coat. But I'm not sure which kind to buy."

"Ewa? A leather coat? What's wrong? Can't you talk?" Eliza asked.

"There are so many coats to choose from here. I don't know which to buy. Could you give me some advice, Eliza?" Ewa kept talking.

Now Eliza knew. Ewa couldn't talk freely. So Eliza said, "OK, some advice . . . if you want to come to Stolberg, it's easy. Get away from your group. Take a bus to the train station. Then take a train to Stolberg. Ewa, if you have money for a ticket there will be no problem.

"There are taxis at the train station. Take one to my apartment. You have my address, right? Don't worry, Ewa. It won't be difficult to get here."

Ewa listened. "Yes, Eliza, that's what I wanted to know." Then Ewa had an idea. Mrs. Ola was listening so she must not say the wrong thing. She spoke carefully.

"Tell me more about that coat, Eliza. It sounds just like what I want. Your friend has a shop? Really? Do you think you could get one for me in Germany? Could you send it to me in Lelystad?"

Ewa looked over at Mrs. Ola again. What was she thinking? Eliza said, "I don't know what you are talking about, Ewa. Do you really want a leather coat?"

Ewa laughed. "No, no, not at all!" she said to Eliza. Then she asked, "Eliza, could you bring the coat here? To Lelystad? We could see each other again! Could you? That would be wonderful. Our last performance is next Thursday . . . yes, Thursday."

This time Eliza asked, "Is this a cover, Ewa? I can't come to Lelystad on Thursday. But you don't really want me to, do you?"

"Yes, that is right," Ewa said. "Oh, I'm so eager to see you again, Eliza! Now let me tell you where the performance will be. . . . Oh, yes, and I must tell you my size." Ewa talked for a few more minutes. Then she said goodbye to Eliza.

Ewa hung up the phone. She looked at Mrs. Ola and said, "Good news. My friend will buy me a coat in Germany for a very good price, so I don't need to buy one here. . . . Well, I'm going back to sleep." And Ewa ran up the stairs.

Chapter 20
Last Performance

Their last performance would begin in 20 minutes. The dancers were warming up behind the stage. Mrs. Ola stood by the door. She was talking to another chaperon.

Ewa pretended to show Tomasz a dance move. "That woman never leaves you, does she?" Tomasz whispered to Ewa.

"Aaaah! I can't stand it," said Ewa softly. "Tomasz, when are we going to try it?" Tomasz could barely hear her whisper.

Their last performance would soon be over. At last Tomasz and Ewa could try to escape. The bus for Poland would leave very late the next night. But when should they try? And how should they do it?

Tomasz looked around the room. No one was near them. He whispered, "At the party tomorrow night. . . . There will be almost 200 people there. Everybody will be drinking. We must wait until the party."

"But that's our last chance. The bus leaves after the party. Are you sure we should wait until then?" Ewa was worried.

"Don't worry, Ewa," whispered Tomasz. "During the day is no good. How will we do it? But the party . . . it's a perfect time!"

There was no more time for talk. It was time for their last performance in Lelystad.

Chapter 21
The Surprise

It was going to be a big party. The dancers, the band, the chaperons, and the families they stayed with were invited. The party was put on by Kasia's uncle's business. Many people from the business would be there too.

Their Dutch family took Ewa and Mrs. Ola in their car. Both women had their suitcases with them. They must be ready to leave for Poland. The bus would leave right after the party.

They drove up to a canal. Ewa enjoyed these lovely channels of water. Canals in the

Netherlands were everywhere. This one was very wide, with a huge boat in the middle of it.

Kasia ran up to their car. "Ewa, look at our party place!" she said. "Out on that boat." Kasia pointed to the boat in the middle of the canal. "Isn't it perfect? Uncle planned it as a surprise for us! I think it's beautiful. What a wonderful way to end our trip!"

Ewa stepped out of the car. She looked at the water on all sides of the boat.

She felt weak. How were she and Tomasz to escape from a boat? She could only swim a little.

Ewa knew Mrs. Ola was watching her. "What a wonderful surprise, Kasia. I must tell your uncle thank you. He has been so kind to us."

A small ferry boat took everyone across the water to the party. Ewa, Kasia, Mrs. Ola, and others waited at the shore. Soon it would be their turn. Ewa felt very sad.

Silently she prayed, "God, are you telling me to return to Poland? Mrs. Ola all week and now this boat. Are these signs that I should go back home?"

Ewa bent her head over the water. Tears filled her eyes. She didn't want anyone to see her cry.

Soon everyone was on the boat. Ewa looked all around for Tomasz. She found him by the food. "Tomasz," she said. She tried to make her voice sound happy. "Will you dance with me?"

The music was slow. Tomasz put his arm around Ewa. "Lead me away from *her*," Ewa whispered. So Tomasz and Ewa danced as far away from Mrs. Ola as they could. "What are we going to do?" said Ewa. "Can you swim?"

"Not at all!" said Tomasz. "I'm scared of the water. Listen, there is just one thing to do. Wait until the party is almost over. Then we will be the first to go back to the bus. We'll grab our bags and run."

"And what about my friend Mrs. Ola?" asked Ewa. "Shall we ask her to go with us?"

"Yes, she's a big problem," said Tomasz. "What do *you* think we should do? Let's hear your idea."

"I need to think for a minute," said Ewa. "There must be a way to get away from Mrs. Ola. Go dance with someone else. Then come ask me to dance again. See you later, Tomasz."

Ewa walked outside on the deck. She looked out at the water. Mrs. Ola was not so close now. She watched Ewa. But she was watching the dance too.

The night was beautiful. The sun was low in the sky. Its golden rays shone on the water. The air was soft and warm. Ewa watched children playing on the shore. Sounds of happy people were all around her.

Ewa felt terribly sad as she thought about the Netherlands. She had heard stories about the West before. But the shops full of things, the well-dressed and well-fed people . . . it was better than she had imagined.

That wasn't all. It wasn't even the most important thing. The people here were free. They said what they wanted. They came and went as they pleased. They lived their lives in the way they chose.

And here she was in the middle of all this freedom. She could not talk freely on the phone. She must explain why she didn't spend her money. She was watched every minute. She couldn't even go back to the bus by herself.

How could a government do this to its people? Cut their telephone lines. Not allow them to travel outside the country. Stop them in the street for no reason. Take away jobs for no reason.

Ewa felt angry. It wasn't fair! Why shouldn't Polish people live freely, like the Dutch people did? Her anger made her stronger. Somehow she *would* escape tonight. She was going to be free. No one would stop her.

Ewa began to pray. "Dear Jesus, I know you suffered much more than me. So you understand my suffering. Please, Jesus, I want to be free. I must be free. Help me escape tonight. Please give me courage. I know you are always with me."

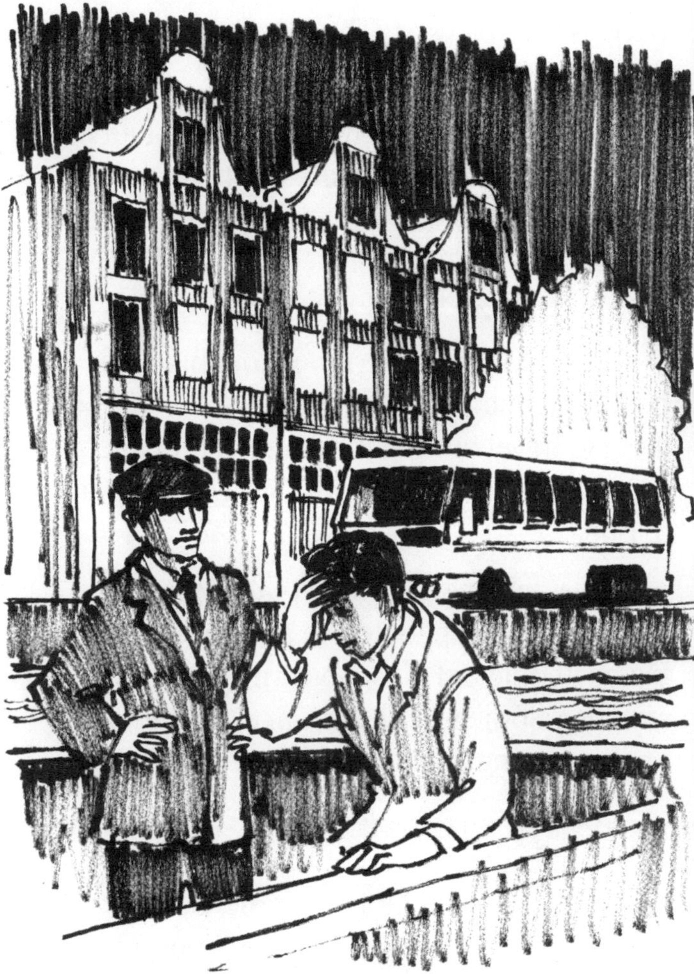

Chapter 22
Ready to Leave

It was 11:00 P.M. The sky was dark at last. And the party was still loud and happy. Ewa and Tomasz were dancing again. They were watching for a good time to leave the party.

Some of the older chaperons were quite drunk. But Mrs. Ola didn't drink. And she was never far from Ewa. But finally she left for a minute. Where was she going? Tomasz and Ewa didn't wait to find out.

Quickly they left the dance floor. Ewa went out one door. Tomasz went out a different door. Tomasz knew just where the ferry boat driver was sitting. Tomasz could not speak Dutch so he made signs with his hands. He pointed to the bus.

Just then the bus driver walked up. "Why do you want to go back to the bus?" he asked. "The party isn't over."

Tomasz put his hand on his head. "I don't feel too good. The music is so loud. My head is aching," he said. "I want to go back a little early. Maybe I'll change my clothes and get comfortable. I really feel terrible. We will go soon, right?"

Ewa stood in the dark a little way away. She could hear Tomasz talking to the bus driver. The bus driver was not going to let Tomasz go. She could hear that. She wished Tomasz would stop talking. He was going to get in trouble.

All night she had been thinking. There simply was no way to get off this boat except to swim. She felt trapped.

A party on a boat! What a surprise! Maybe if she understood more Dutch she would have heard about it. Then she could have tried to escape a different way. Now it was too late.

The bus driver was still talking. "No one goes back until Mrs. Ola says so. Go sit down if you're sick. And stop drinking! This party isn't over yet."

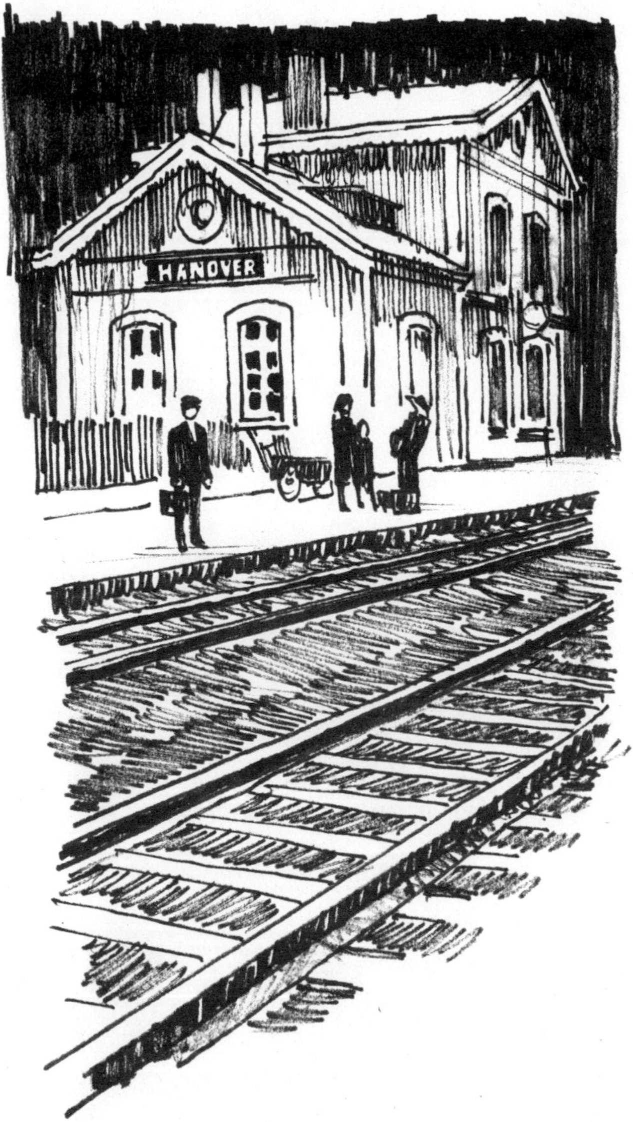
HANOVER

Chapter 23
Bus Ride to Poland

It was after midnight. Everyone in the group said goodbyes to their new Dutch friends. "Thank you! Thank you!" they called from the bus. It was time to go.

Mrs. Ola walked up and down. Yes, everyone was here. She smiled as the bus started. It was time to leave the Netherlands. And no one had tried to defect.

Ewa looked out the window. Only one time had she felt sadder than she did now. That was when her mother was dying. Like then, she felt hopeless now. The bus would not stop in West Germany. It would only stop when they got to Germany, a Communist country.

As the bus drove away from the canal, everyone laughed and talked. What a wonderful trip it had been. There was so much to tell people in Poland. Some dancers began drinking. Others started singing. But Ewa just looked out the window.

Mile after mile. Ewa watched the signs for one Dutch city after another. Soon they would leave the Netherlands and enter West Germany.

Ewa felt angry at Tomasz. Why did they wait until the party to escape? But how could they have escaped during the day? She would have had to go alone. But when? And where?

Ewa laid her head back on the seat and sighed. She felt angry at God too. She needed his help. But everything had gone wrong. God must want her to go back to Poland.

"But I can't go back!" she cried inside. "Dear God, I know you are here with me," she prayed. "Please make this bus stop. Let us run out of gas, break down, anything! Oh God, help me. I have to be free. I can't go back to Poland!"

Then Ewa waited for a minute. "But, God, I accept your will for me. If it must be, I will go back to Poland." She shook her head. What else could she say? It was not her choice now.

The bus was speeding through West Germany. Everyone quieted down. Soon many fell asleep. Ewa still looked out the window.

Ewa heard someone crying near the front of the bus. A woman from the band got up. She walked back to Mrs. Ola.

"I have to use a bathroom," she cried softly. "I have terrible cramps. Please can we stop? I can't wait much longer." There was pain in her voice.

Ewa tried to listen. But Mrs. Ola and two other chaperons were whispering. It was hard for Ewa to hear. The sick woman walked back to her seat. She was still crying.

Mrs. Ola talked to the chaperons sitting behind Ewa. Ewa closed her eyes like she was sleeping. Mrs. Ola said, "I don't think we should stop. She can wait until East Germany."

One of the chaperons said, "Well, I have some business in Hanover. I need to make a few phone calls. Let's stop in the train station there. Everyone can use the bathroom. We'll get gas too. It will only take an hour."

The chaperons whispered some more. Then Mrs. Ola went to the front of the bus. She talked to two more chaperons. Then she talked to the bus driver. By now the sick woman was crying hard.

Hanover was still in West Germany! A free country. Ewa prayed the same prayer over and over. "Please, God, may we stop. May we stop! Oh, may we stop! Let us stop in Hanover. Oh please, dear God . . . "

Chapter 24
Last Stop

The bus did stop in Hanover. The sick woman and her chaperon got off first. Then the others got off. Many had been sound asleep.

Ewa and Tomasz were almost the last. They walked toward the train station. They did not look at each other. Ewa had her purse. But her bag was still on the bus. Mrs. Ola was ahead of them. She kept looking back at Ewa. Her face was hard. She wanted no problems in Hanover.

Ewa walked ahead of Tomasz. They were thinking the same thing. But they didn't dare talk to each other. They didn't dare look at each other. They both knew this was their last chance.

"Maybe I'll look in the shops here, if they are open," Ewa said to Mrs. Ola. She yawned.

"I'll go with you," said Mrs. Ola. "But I don't think they'll have leather coats here." She looked at Ewa. "Your friend never did come with that coat."

Ewa's heart pounded. "Yes, it's too bad," she answered. "I wonder what happened to Eliza. She never even called me.

"Oh well, maybe I'll spend some money here. But first I need to use the bathroom." Ewa said it loud so Tomasz could hear. He was walking close behind them.

"I need to use the bathroom too," said Mrs. Ola. They walked toward the restrooms. Mrs. Ola went first.

Ewa followed her. Before she walked in, she looked back at Tomasz. She gave her head a little nod. Then she walked in.

A German woman was in the bathroom to help. "Right this way, ma'am," she said to Mrs. Ola. She wiped off a toilet seat. She held the door for Mrs. Ola to go in. Then she turned to Ewa. "And you, Miss, right over here." And the woman bent to clean another toilet seat.

When the German woman looked up, Ewa was gone.

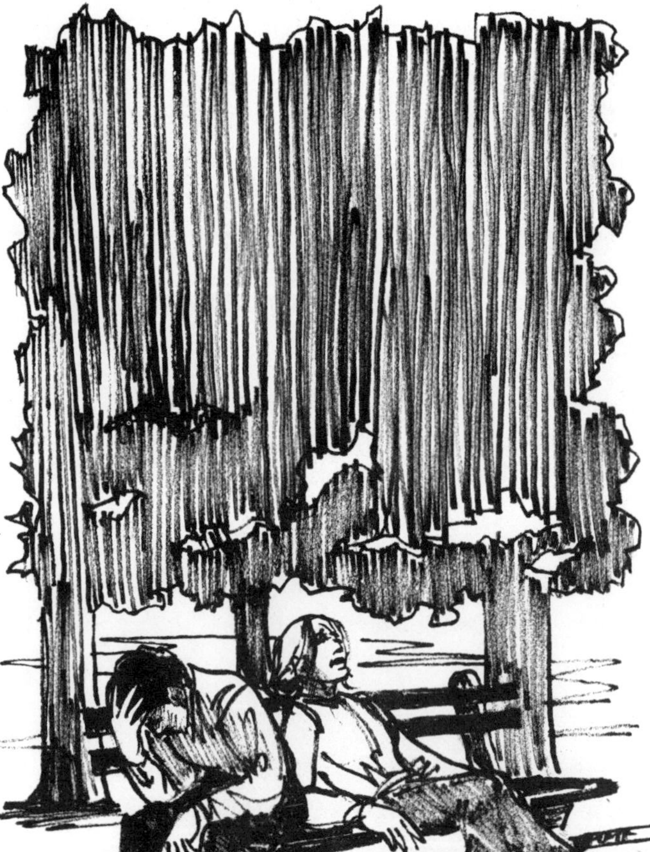

Chapter 25
A New Day

Tomasz and Ewa ran and ran. Down one street and then another. The sky was just getting light. Because it was so early, there were few people outside.

Ewa was sure her lungs would burst. Her legs felt heavy and tired. But she forced herself to keep running. On and on. They must not stop, not even for a second. Somehow Ewa must run as fast as Tomasz.

A terrible fear filled Ewa. She looked behind her. Were the Communists following them? A police car drove by. Tomasz and Ewa slowed down. Would the car stop? Were the German police looking for them? But the car kept going.

Ewa looked at the people they passed. Could they see that she and Tomasz were Polish defectors? She had seen people in the Netherlands running for exercise. Yes, she must act relaxed. People must think she and Tomasz were out for a morning run.

Suddenly Ewa felt confused. Did Tomasz know where he was going? Were they going the right way? What if they were running back to the train station? But Tomasz seemed sure. All she could do was follow him.

It was getting lighter. Now they were half running, half walking. Ewa knew she was making Tomasz go slower. But she could not go any faster.

More people were on the streets now. Two young women looked at Tomasz and Ewa with surprise. Suddenly Ewa knew why. It was their clothes.

She and Tomasz wore long-sleeved shirts, blue jeans, and leather shoes. Runners wore shorts, T-shirts, and running shoes. Fear filled Ewa again. They must stop soon. They must get off the streets.

Tomasz pointed ahead to a large area of green trees. Ewa forced herself to run faster. Salty sweat ran down her face. It was burning her eyes. Her feet burned too. They must stop soon.

Ten minutes later they reached the park. There was a grassy area with many paths. On one side Ewa saw a play area for children. There were also many areas filled with flowers. Just ahead was a large area of trees, a woods.

Ewa and Tomasz walked quickly down the path to the woods. They stopped when they got there. They were breathing so hard they couldn't talk. Ewa looked at Tomasz. He looked terrible. His clothes were soaked with sweat. His eyes looked red.

Tomasz was stronger than Ewa. But he had drunk a lot of vodka that night. Some at the party and more on the bus. Now he felt as bad as he looked.

Ewa pointed. Just ahead was a stream. They walked to it. They found a place where the trees were thick. No one else was around. They cupped their hands and dipped them in the cool water. They drank and drank.

Finally, they splashed their faces. Still they didn't speak. Their hearts pounded. Their lungs hurt as they tried to get enough air.

"Look . . . a bench." Thomasz pointed. The bench was hidden in the trees. "Let's go over there and rest."

Ewa nodded her head. But first she looked all around. Had the Communists followed them? She saw no one.

Ewa and Tomasz flopped on the bench. Tomasz groaned with pain. But then he smiled at Ewa. "We did it, Ewa! We're free. We are *free* people!"

Ewa was breathing better now. The same happiness filled her! She hugged Tomasz. "I don't believe it. The bus stopped! The bus really stopped in West Germany. Oh, Tomasz, that bus almost took us back to Poland!"

Then Ewa laughed. "Tomasz, you may dance like an elephant . . . but you run like a deer! Oh my poor, poor aching legs."

Tomasz laughed with her. "I learned all those dances . . . *all* those dances . . . and it was almost for nothing. We were almost back to Poland. I was so depressed on the bus. . . . I thought we had failed."

"Me too," answered Ewa. "But then Anna . . . dear sick little Anna. She got stomach cramps. I couldn't believe the bus would stop in West Germany! Now here we are, Tomasz. Are we dreaming?"

Ewa and Tomasz talked for a long time. They talked about the party, the bus ride, Mrs. Ola, the long run. Could it be? Were they really free? Yes, it was not a dream! But Ewa was still a little worried. Was there any way Mrs. Ola could still find them?

Tomasz felt a terrible tiredness come over him. "I've got to sleep now . . . just for a little while," he said. Slowly he lay down on the bench. Ewa moved off the bench and sat on the grass. "Just . . . just a . . . little nap," he said. And he was asleep.

Ewa looked at him and shook her head. Too much vodka on the bus. She was glad he could still run so far. She rested her back on the bench. With Tomasz sleeping, she felt afraid again.

She watched the park beyond the trees. It was getting busy. Several Germans hurried down a path. They looked like they were going to work. And there was a mother pushing her baby in a cart. But there were no Polish Communists. No Mrs. Ola.

Then Ewa remembered her prayers on the bus. She must not forget to thank God. "Oh, dear God," she said, "you answered my prayers. It was a miracle the bus stopped. Thank you! Thank you so very much. Oh, God, thank you."

Tears came quickly as she prayed some more. "I need courage. Don't let me be afraid. I know you are with me. Whatever happens you are with me. Oh, God, thank you for freedom. Now give me courage to go on."

Then Ewa thought about the bus. It would return to Poland without her. She thought about Papa waiting for her at home. He would be confused and unhappy when she didn't come home.

"Please help Papa to understand," she prayed. "Dear God, take care of Papa . . . and Adam and Grazyna and the baby. They need you just like I do." Strong feelings almost choked her. Pain for Papa, fear of the Communists, thankfulness. So many feelings.

Ewa felt very, very tired. She lay down on the grass near the bench. Suddenly she sat up. Were those Polish voices she heard? She looked all around. But no, it was Germans in the park . . . a long way from her . . . not Mrs. Ola or the others.

Once again she looked around. The morning was still cool. But the sun was warming the flowers. The birds were singing in the trees. The stream nearby sparkled. The air smelled sweet and fresh. There was beauty wherever she looked.

Ewa lay down again on the cool, prickly grass. God had taken her to this place. She must believe that he would keep her safe.

She closed her eyes. Her mind was full of thoughts . . . of Poland, of Mama and Papa, of the Netherlands, of the run to the park. . . . Then she was asleep.

Epilogue

At the train station, the Communists looked for Ewa and Tomasz. They searched the station. They searched the nearby streets. The bus stayed in Hanover for four hours while they searched. Then it returned to Poland without them.

Tomasz and Ewa spent most of the day in Hanover. Late that afternoon, they went to a different train station. They took a train to Dartmouth where Tomasz's aunt lived. Two days later, Ewa said goodbye to Tomasz. She took a train to Stolberg to find her friend Eliza.